THE V
STU
Sporting
Screw-Ups

THE WORLD'S STUPIDEST
Sporting
Screw-Ups

Andrew John
and
Stephen Blake

Michael O'Mara Humour

First published in Great Britain in 2004 by
Michael O'Mara Books Limited
9 Lion Yard
Tremadoc Road
London SW4 7NQ

Previously published in hardback in 2002 as *Sporting Slip-Ups and Goalmouth
Gaffes* by Michael O'Mara Books Limited

A CIP catalogue record for this book is available from the British Library

ISBN 1-84317-039-6

1 3 5 7 9 10 8 6 4 2

Designed and typeset by Design 23

Printed and bound in Great Britain by Cox & Wyman, Reading, Berks.

Contents

Introduction

Sport should be fun, even when it's being taken deadly seriously. In fact, that's when it's the most fun, because it's when the deadly serious get their comeuppance or their pride bubble is burst that we tend to laugh the most.

We've all had that sense of *schadenfreude* when a sportsman who's been doing so well throws it all away on the last hole or the last penalty shot, the final furlong or the last lap. Not all the stories in our collection feature such mishaps, but there are plenty that do. Some reveal plain foolishness, some bad luck. Some are funny, others just interesting in a quirky sort of way. *The World's Stupidest Sporting Screw-Ups* takes a light-hearted look at things that have gone wrong in the world of sport; a collection of events that might otherwise be forgotten.

We have found stories in a variety of ways – trawling through books and records, surfing the Internet, talking to sporting friends, reading newspapers and magazines – and have enjoyed bringing to you some of the wackier moments of sport, such as when the autograph-signing famous golfer found himself pushed into the lake by adoring fans; when a US president's golf ball hit a woman spectator between the eyes, shattering her glasses; when a famous racing driver pulled down an awning on to his boss's head because he had forgotten to unhook the air line as he set off for the starting grid, and the story of the football team that ended the season with minus one point.

Our collection of stories spans three centuries, featuring some celebrated tales, and some not so well known, from the nineteenth century through to the present day. We hope you will find them as entertaining and amusing as we do.

Andrew John and Stephen Blake

On Track and Field

There is nothing like the Olympic or Commonwealth Games to rouse our national spirit. Whether in track or field events, we are all rooting for 'our' woman and man out there, jumping, sprinting, throwing a javelin or putting a shot.

Here is our own 'running' commentary on some of the wackier moments in the history of athletics.

And the winner is . . . the loser

The men's 400-yards final at the 1938 Empire Games in Sydney was such a close race that it caused an unprecedented toing and froing of the coveted prize.

After a fifteen-minute wait, England's Bill Roberts and Canadian Bill Fritz finally heard the officials' verdict. Initially they declared that Roberts had crossed the line first. But after another discussion it was announced that another decision had been reached – Fritz was the winner.

Canadians began celebrating, but their joy was short-lived. Officials gathered once more and mumbled among themselves. They then announced the winner for the final time – it was Roberts again!

Dogged determination

At the 1950 Empire Games in Auckland, New Zealand, forty-three-year-old Jack Holden of England won the marathon, despite having had to remove his running shoes, which had been soaked by a sudden downpour, and complete the course barefoot.

What had made his win even more surprising, however, was the distracting presence of a pesky dog that had insisted on following him, in spite of his polite attempts to tell the irksome canine where to go. At one point the dog nearly tripped him up, until race officials managed to guide it away.

Everyone's a winner, baby

Australia's Gary Holdsworth was asked to hand over the bronze medal he had won – or thought he had won – for the men's 100-yards race in the 1962 Commonwealth Games in Perth. Some days after the event, an appeals jury looked at a print of the finish and decided that the third place had not been won by Holdsworth but by his teammate, Mike Cleary.

Holdsworth was quoted as shouting at officials, 'You've got to be joking, haven't you? My time was listed faster.'

Oddly enough, photographic evidence had not been called for on the day, but a photograph had been taken, and it was this that led the appeals jury to make their final decision. It showed that Cleary was 5 centimetres (2 inches) ahead of his fellow Australian. As a compromise, however, both men were awarded a bronze medal.

Going with the wind

In 1960, at the West German Athletics Championships, Manfred Steinbach would have been just a centimetre short of Jesse Owens's world-record, 8.15-metre long jump, which had stood since 1935.

Steinbach's fourth leap measured 8.14 metres, but the official in charge, Walter Blume, announced that the following wind was 3.2 metres per second. That was 1.2 metres per second higher than the permissible level of 2.0, and so the distance was not recorded.

Blume later admitted, however, that he had not had a wind gauge working for that particular jump, and rather than admit to such a major professional oversight, he gave a wind speed that would have rendered the record invalid. Adding to Steinbach's frustration, it emerged that the wind on all his other jumps that day was not above 1.1 metres per second.

It's a lock-out

During the 1979 Pan American Games in San Juan in Puerto Rico, Wallace Williams of the Virgin Islands was trailing by about thirty-nine minutes when the runner in front of him had entered the stadium.

By the time poor Wallace had arrived at the stadium, he found it was locked. Everybody had gone home.

Rarin' to go

Exhibiting the highest level of hearty sporting enthusiasm, a supremely keen pack of runners in the Boston marathon in 1900 produced an extraordinary false start.

There were a large number of Canadian

runners in the field who were so full of adrenalin and ready to race that, as soon as the starter, John Graham, had finished his official speech, but before he could formally start the race, off they sprinted.

Keep your eye on that one, Boyd

Excuses, excuses! Probably the most original one came from the American 400-metre hurdler Boyd Gittins, who was taking part in the 1968 Olympic trials in the United States.

Gittins's reason for being eliminated was that a pigeon dropping had hit him in the eye and one of his contact lenses had been dislodged just as he was about to take the first hurdle.

Lap of dishonour (1)

Sometimes it is possible to achieve gold in spite of a sporting screw-up, as New Zealand's Billy Savidan discovered.

The occasion was the 1930 Empire Games at Hamilton in Canada, and a track official made a blunder by turning over one card too many on the counter that tells runners how many laps are remaining.

When Savidan thought he was on the last lap, he was not. After he had sprinted down the home straight, he was told he still had a lap to run. He had stopped running at this point and seemed not to believe what he was being told.

Once the awful truth was confirmed for him, he had no option but to carry on, and with an amazing last-ditch effort, he managed to complete the final lap – the real final lap – and win gold, with England's Ernest Harper in hot pursuit. Savidan collapsed in the dressing room before he received his medal.

Then, after all the fuss surrounding the event, the band played the English anthem, 'Land of Hope and Glory', instead of the New Zealand anthem.

Lap of dishonour (2)

During a competition between Africa and the United States in 1971, the Ethiopian runner Miruts Yifter thought he was on the last lap and had all but used his last ounce of energy to cross the finishing line, only to discover that it was actually the penultimate lap.

Having thoroughly exhausted himself, all Yifter could do was jog around the last lap, leaving it to Steve Prefontaine of the United States to run past him and win the race.

Success went to his head

James Trapp, from Clemson University in the United States, had a dizzying moment after coming third in a 200-metres college event, when he was bashed over the head with the trophy.

The winner of the race, Dave Braunskill, had lifted the trophy aloft in triumph following his victory, but Trapp's head got in the way and needed several stitches.

Majestic throw

Whether royalist or republican, it is simply not acceptable to go around throwing hammers at members of the royal family, unless one wishes to spend the rest of one's days languishing in the Tower.

Queen Elizabeth II must have been in a good mood at the 1978 Commonwealth Games at Edmonton, therefore, when a hammer came hurtling above the heads of photographers and landed not far from her, narrowly missing a CBS cameraman during its wayward journey. Officials decided that the hammer competition would be better postponed until after the royal party had left the stadium.

The Games were next held in Canada in 1994. When organizers were asked on which day they would prefer to hold the hammer event, they replied, 'Any day the Queen isn't there.'

The dizziness of the long-distance runner

A sense of direction is rather important to a runner. It helps to be able to find one's way to the finish line, after all.

However, during the marathon in the 1954 European Championships in Berne, Ivan Filin of Russia had just overtaken Finland's Veikko Karvonen, and stormed into the stadium, certain to win.

But then he went that way and ran for more than a hundred metres before he realized he should have gone this way. Or was it the other way? Whichever way, he ended up finishing third.

Milk of unkindness

When Samuel Ferris of Great Britain was out on a training run to familiarize himself with the course of the 1932 Olympic marathon in Los Angeles, he decided he would use a huge milk advertisement as a marker for his final effort, about a mile (1.6 km) from the finish.

On race day, however, he did not see his marker. In front of the advertisement a grandstand had been erected, so poor old Ferris's view was obscured. He did not win either, and he got the silver instead of the gold he had expected to achieve. He was a full minute behind the winner Juan Carlos Zabala of Argentine, when he entered the stadium.

Not for the high jump

In the 1912 Olympic high jump in Stockholm, Germany's
Hans Liesche had to jump 6 feet 4 inches (1.9 metres) to
equal the best effort of the United States' Alma Richards.

Having already had two failures at the height, Liesche
was entitled to only one more attempt. With great
concentration, he composed himself and prepared for his
moment, but was thwarted by the loud bang of a gun,
signalling the start of a track race.

Liesche had to wait for the race to end before he could
prepare himself mentally to try again. The moment he
had regained his composure, the stadium band began to
play and Liesche's nerves were in tatters.

Knowing he could not hold
back for much longer (indeed,
a Swedish official had already
told him to hurry), he
completed his run and jump
half-heartedly, resulting in a
dismal failure for the
unfortunate German.

Pardon my French

Loren Murchison of the United States was in a state of
confusion at the beginning of the 1920 Olympic men's 100-
metres final because of a translation problem.

The Games were being held in Antwerp, Belgium, and
the starter was speaking French. When he said 'Prêt',
Murchison thought the competitors had been told to stand
up, though literally the word means 'ready', that is 'get set'
within the context of a race.

However, Murchison was relaxing his body and getting to
his feet when 'Bang!' – off went the starting pistol. The
American trailed his fellow competitors by 9 metres (10
yards), and came last.

Pot luck

It was the occasion of the 4,000-metres cross-country, the final event of the modern pentathlon during the 1984 Olympic Games in Los Angeles, and Svante Rasmusson of Sweden had pulled clear. However, just 18 metres (20 yards) from the finish, he fell over a potted plant that had been put there to brighten up the course.

Unfortunately for Rasmusson, it did not brighten his day. Before he could get back on his feet, Italy's Daniele Masala shot past him and won gold.

The heat was off for Wym

It turned out to be a wasted journey for Wym Essajas of Surinam (formerly Dutch Guiana, in South America) when he became the first person to be chosen to represent his country in the 1960 Olympic Games in Rome. He had been due to take part in the men's 800-metre race, but a breakdown in communications had ruined his chances.

Wym had been told that the heats were taking place in the afternoon, but in actual fact they were scheduled for the morning.

Naturally, he had spent the morning resting and mentally preparing for the heats, only to find that, on arrival at the stadium, they had already taken place.

So he returned to Surinam, having missed the opportunity to make Olympic Games history for his country.

We have ignition – but then again . . .

Sheffield-born Helen Sharman was Britain's first astronaut and, when athletics organizers needed a celebrity to take part in the opening ceremony of the World Student Games in Sheffield in 1991, Sharman was the natural choice.

Perhaps she was still feeling the effects of weightlessness

after her travels in space, for Sharman, who was to perform the symbolic job of lighting the flame to declare the Games open, managed to trip on a red carpet in the stadium, and dropped the flaming torch, extinguishing it completely.

Silver bubbles

There were just two miles to go for Charles Hefferon of South Africa in the 1908 London Olympic marathon, when he made the fateful decision to accept a drink of champagne.

The bubbly did not give him the fizz required to strike gold; on the contrary, it made him disoriented and eventually gave him stomach cramps.

But he did manage to win a silver medal.

That's our race!

It must have been quite disconcerting to be watching television only to see athletes lining up to begin the race in which you were supposed to be taking part. It happened during the 1972 Munich Olympics, when two American runners, Eddie Hart and Rey Robinson, were among the favourites to win the men's 100-metres race.

Frustratingly, the athletes never arrived, thanks to their coach who had misread the starting time. So, as they watched television while waiting for the team bus at the Olympic village, Robinson was horrified to see athletes lining up for the race that he had been expected to win.

What a splashing fellow!

While Sergei Skrypka of the Soviet Union was competing in a heat of the 3,000-metres steeplechase in the 1972 Olympic Games in Munich, he managed to lose one of his shoes.

There were six laps to go and, despite his half-shod status, Skrypka managed to keep up with the leaders.

But on the final water jump, Sergei's bare foot slipped on the wet barrier, and sent him plummeting headlong into the water.

Taking the Flack

Australia's Edwin Flack was exhausted by the time he was less than 5 km (3 miles) from the finishing line during the 1896 Olympic marathon in Athens.

So tired was he that he seemed likely to collapse into an ungainly heap, until someone asked a Greek spectator to help him. In his delirious state, however, Flack thought the spectator was about to attack him, and he punched the helpful chap to the ground.

Flack decided to retire from the race after that.

Traffic hold-up

In the 1984 Olympic women's marathon in Los Angeles, Honduran athlete Leda Diaz de Cano had become separated from the rest of the runners. In fact she was so far behind the other competitors – a total of 27 minutes,

20 km (12.4 miles) – that officials had to persuade her to retire so they could reopen the streets to traffic.

Far-flung

Records were not the only things broken at an athletics event held in north-east England in 1952.

The hammer thrower twirled his hammer around, let go, and off it went, landing outside the enclosure, right on the bonnet of his own Triumph Spitfire, which he had arranged to sell that night. He had to spend £150 to fix the damage.

The hammer's journey had only just begun, for after bouncing off the bonnet of the car, it went straight through the window of the stadium office, knocking an official unconscious.

It was not the first time that the hammer thrower had caused such havoc; previously he had hit a petrol station, a gents' toilet – from which a spectator emerged hurriedly, thinking it had been struck by lightning – and a police car.

Unseen, unsung

The stupidity of the American officials at the 1932 Olympic Games in Los Angeles is very hard to beat. John Anderson of the United States was leading the men's discus competition, and when Jules Noël of France launched his fourth throw, it appeared to land ahead of Anderson's leading distance.

Unfortunately, the officials were all watching a pole vault close by, and did not see where Noël's throw had landed.

Offered another throw as compensation, Noël was unable to repeat the disputed performance, and missed out on a crucial opportunity to challenge for top spot.

Right on the button

During the 1950 Empire Games, spectators were baffled by the behaviour of the South African hurdler Tom Lavery who, during the final of the 120-yard hurdles event, was holding up his shorts by the waist.

It transpired that a button had come loose and fallen from his shorts as soon as he started to run. If he had not held them up, not only would he have faced embarrassment, but he would also have tripped up and landed on his face.

Despite his unfortunate handicap, he won bronze.

And the band played on

At the Helsinki Olympics in 1952 no one had expected Luxembourg to win gold, and so no one had given the band the score for the country's national anthem.

Luxembourg did win gold in the men's 1,500-metres final, however, through their runner Josef Barthel.

At the medal ceremony, the band had to improvise, and nobody noticed the difference.

Dogged by bad luck

A dog is not always a man's best friend – especially when that man is trying to win a marathon.

The events of 1961 proved this to be the case when John J. Kelley of the United States was almost level with Eino Oksanen of Finland during the 1961 Boston marathon. As the two men battled it out, a stray dog decided to join in, unaware of how important the race was for his two-legged fellow runners, who had to keep breaking stride as the dog impeded their progress.

Eventually, 27 km (17 miles) into the race, Kelley fell over the clumsy canine and needed to be helped to his feet by another runner. The incident cost him valuable time and ultimately the race, because he finished second – just fifteen seconds behind the Finn.

Yifter's eight-year wait

If you want to get ahead, avoid getting stuck in the loo. It happened to the Ethiopian distance runner Miruts Yifter ('Yifter the Shifter', as he was better known) in the 1972 Munich Olympics. He missed the start of a 5,000-metres heat because he was in the toilet, and could not reach the track in time.

Ethiopia boycotted the 1976 Olympics so Yifter had to wait eight years to have another attempt at winning the 5,000-metres gold. In 1980 he eventually claimed his crown.

Country style

During the Olympic cross-country event in 1924, which was run over a distance of 10,000 metres (6.2 miles), the competitors began dropping like flies.

Not only was it a very hot day in Paris, but some of the runners were overcome by noxious fumes coming from a nearby energy plant. If that were not enough, parts of the circuit were covered with knee-high thistles.

There were mishaps, too. When Aguilar of Spain entered the stadium he hit his head on a marker. Sewell of Great Britain had headed off in the wrong direction and had to be told which way to run. Having been thus redirected, he banged into a fellow runner. Both men fell and did not finish the course. Paavo Nurmi of Finland got the gold, the first of only fifteen competitors to complete the race from a starting line-up of thirty-eight.

A walk on the wildly expensive side

It was an expensive way to win the 50-km walk, but Don Thompson of Great Britain decided that to be fully prepared, he needed to acclimatize himself. It would be hot in Rome in the 1960 Olympic Games, and so Don converted his bathroom into a sauna by turning up the gas to its highest level.

During the eighteen months before the Games he sat, or probably marked time, in his bathroom to get used to the sweltering heat and, in the process, notched up a gas bill of £9,763.

When he returned from his Olympic triumph, he discovered the gas board had cut him off.

Winner's loss

The Russian athlete Ivanov Vyacheslav was thrilled to win a medal at the 1956 Melbourne Olympics. He was so thrilled, in fact, that in his excitement he threw the medal high into the air. It landed in Lake Wendouree, and was never found.

Clang!

When you drop a clanger, it is advisable not to do it front of millions of spectators, both in the stadium and across the world glued to television sets, but it happened at the start of the final lap of a 5,000-metres heat during the 1978 Commonwealth Games.

The official tolled the bell to signal the final lap, and the bell responded by falling off its stand in a most undignified manner.

Do share my lunch

France's Joseph Guillemot was not feeling too well. During the 1920 Olympic Games in Antwerp, the king of Belgium had requested that the 10,000-metres race be brought forward from 5.30 p.m. to 2.15 p.m.

Unfortunately Guillemot had not been informed of the change in timing, and had just eaten a hearty lunch. So, when Paavo Nurmi won the race, Guillemot – who was the runner-up – was sick all over Nurmi's shoes.

Ripe for failure

A Cuban postman named Feliz Carvajal was taking part in the 1904 Olympic marathon, but lost out on a medal position after a spot of tummy trouble.

It was his own fault, however, as he had stopped to talk to some spectators en route, and had eaten some unripe fruit. The resulting indigestion caused him to finish in fourth place.

Fast track to frustration (1)

'I laughed, but I felt like crying,' said South Africa's Johannes Coleman after being told his new world record could not be ratified. 'It must have been my fastest ever marathon.'

The occasion was the 1938 Natal marathon at Alexander Park, Pietermaritzburg. The world record at the time stood at 2 hours, 26 minutes and 42 seconds. As he entered the park at the end of his run, Coleman's own watch indicated that he had completed the race in 2 hours and 23 minutes.

He went in search of Harold Sulin, the chief timekeeper, to confirm his score, but found him with colleagues drinking tea in the refreshment room. They were most apologetic, admitting that no one had expected Coleman or any of the runners to finish the race so quickly. So the record could not be ratified.

Fast track to frustration (2)

Runners were told to go the wrong way when they entered the stadium at the end of the 1912 Polytechnic Harriers marathon in London. Instead of the 840 yards they would have run, they only completed 480 yards.

Unfortunately for James Corkery of Canada, who thought he had achieved a world record, he was told his time could not be recognized because it was short of the full marathon distance.

A celebrated defeat

Alex Wilson of Canada was sure he had achieved victory in the men's 800-metres final during the 1932 Olympic Games in Los Angeles. So sure, in fact, that he threw up his arms while still a yard from the finish. His celebratory gesture proved to be premature, however, for as he eased his speed a little, while his hands were in the air, Britain's Tommy Hampson put on a final spurt, and went past him. Wilson was fated never to win Olympic gold.

Beware of Greeks blowing trumpets

The United States team thought they had got everything nicely planned when they set off for the 1896 Olympics in Athens (the last time they were held there, incidentally, before 2004). They spent between sixteen and seventeen days at sea, and thought, when they arrived in Athens on 5 April, that they had another twelve days before the Games began.

However, they had not realized that Greece was still using the Julian calendar, and was eleven days ahead; and so the Americans got a nasty surprise when, after the end of their long journey, they awoke to the sound of a brass band proclaiming the commencement of the Games.

Contraflow on legs

Confusion reigned at the end of the 1946 Amateur Athletic Association marathon at the White City stadium in London, when Squire Yarrow and Donald McNab Robertson stormed on to the track.

A steeplechase was still in progress, and so the marathon runners had to dodge hurdles, not to mention other runners. They managed it, however, and Yarrow got there just ahead of Robertson.

Your Ringside Seat

With its charmless machismo, it could be thought that an activity such as boxing, in which the object is to batter one's opponent into submission, would be the last sport to bring forth amusement and mirth. This has proved not to be the case, however, as the following pages contain a number of knockout stories, guaranteed to raise a smile.

Caught napping

The occasion of the world middleweight title fight between Billy Papke and the challenger, George Bernard of France, in Paris in December 1912, produced one of the more unusual endings to a fight in boxing history. There was no knockout or a win on points. In fact, it was all rather anti-climactic.

Between the sixth and seventh rounds Bernard fell into a deep sleep in his corner, and his team could not rouse him in time to begin fighting again. So Papke was declared the winner and Bernard 'retired'.

It was later claimed that the fight had been rigged and the boxer himself claimed he had been doped.

I'm sitting this one out

When the Korean flyweight Choh Dong-kih was disqualified for holding his head too low after just over a minute of the first round of a quarter-final fight during the 1964 Tokyo Olympics, he refused to accept the decision.

He was so angry, in fact, that he sat on the canvas, right in the middle of the ring, and refused to move. He remained there for fifty-one minutes before officials persuaded him to end his protest.

KO'd by emotion

Clement Quartey of Ghana did not expect to win the light-welterweight final at the 1962 Commonwealth Games in Perth. Everyone seemed convinced that Scotland's Dick McTaggart would be the victor on points.

So, when the judges awarded their decision in favour of Quartey, he was so overcome that he fainted, and was out cold on the canvas – an unusual position for a winner to find himself – for about five minutes following the announcement of his victory.

More refs than fighters

Boxing referees have to be nimble on their feet, but this is to ensure they can see the fight from all angles, not to avoid blows. After all, the fighters are usually good at aiming their fists at each other, and so referees do not expect to be punched in the face. However, during a heavyweight fight held at Leicester's Granby Halls, not one, but two referees became caught in the crossfire.

Punches were flying in the ring as the two heavyweights battled to get the upper hand, and as a result of a wayward punch that landed on the hapless referee's chin, the poor man hit the canvas. Not quite knocked out, he was in no condition to continue his duties on the night. A substitute was called for, but in his enthusiasm to replace his injured colleague, the second referee tripped as he ran up the corner steps and twisted an ankle.

The bout was almost certain to be postponed until the boxing manager, George Biddles, stepped into the ring to referee the remaining rounds. Fortunately, he came to no harm, as seconds later, one of the boxers landed a knockout punch, and all Biddles had to do was count to ten.

Revealing gesture

Richard Procter, a featherweight boxer, gave his audience more than they had bargained for when he stepped smartly into the ring at the World Sporting Club in London.

Coolly he slipped off his gown and, with some aplomb, threw it into the corner to an outburst of raucous cheering. It took a few seconds for him to realize that the sudden burst of shouting, applauding and whistling was not in appreciation of his fighting prowess – after all, the bout had yet to begin. Only when he looked down did he realize he had left his shorts in the dressing room.

The bells, the bells

During the Seoul Olympics in 1988, a possible boxing knockout turned into a farce, and all because of ringing bells.

In making the decision to stage more than one fight at a time in one hall, officials had not considered the effect that the noise of more than one bell would have. How would a fighter know whether the bell he heard ringing was for his own fight or someone else's?

The inevitable happened during a light-welterweight

fight between Todd Foster of the United States and
Chun Jin Chul from South Korea.

Chun heard a bell and thought it referred to his own
bout. Understandably, he began to walk to his corner.
However, the bell had been from another fight. Foster
then took advantage of the muddle, and delivered a
powerful left hook to the unsuspecting Chun, knocking
him to the canvas. The referee even began to count, but
then seemed to realize that a mistake had been made.
Confusion descended within the ring, and ultimately the
judges decided it should be restaged the following day.
Foster won the re-match.

Thumbs down

John Coker, a lightweight boxer from Sierra Leone, was
due to take up a place in the 1966 Empire and
Commonwealth Games in Kingston, Jamaica.

Unfortunately, Coker had exceptionally long thumbs,
and despite endless searches, he could not find a pair of
gloves to fit. As a result, he was deemed to be
improperly equipped and was duly disqualified.

Weighty decision

It was a great honour for the small Pacific island of
Vanuatu when it sent its only representative to the 1988
Olympics in Los Angeles. Eduard Paululum was the
island's first Olympic competitor.

Over-excited and carried away with the celebrations, he
mistakenly ate a hearty breakfast before his first-round
weigh-in, and was found to be just a pound overweight.
In accordance with the rules he was disqualified and had
to return home without having thrown a single punch.

Out – and out

Jack Doyle, the battling Irishman, ended up the loser, despite being the favourite, when he found himself stuck outside the ring.

He was taking on Eddie Phillips in a heavyweight bout at Harringay in London in September 1938, and during the second round Doyle flew at Phillips, but missed him and continued on, through the ropes and out of the ring.

The referee began the count, but Doyle could not get back in time, and was counted out. Phillips was the surprise – and surprised – victor.

Photo finish

Adolpho Washington had already suffered a cut eye during his WBA light-heavyweight title fight against the defender Virgil Hill in February 1993.

After the eleventh round at Fargo, North Dakota, Washington was having his eye checked by a doctor at the ringside, when an overenthusiastic cameraman went in for a good close-up. In his excitement, the cameraman hit Washington's eye with his camera, and it began to bleed even more. Consequently, Washington was unable to continue.

Seconds away

At just half a second long, it must have been the shortest fight on record. It was ten and a half seconds, more accurately, but ten of those comprised the count following Ralph Walton's knockout by Al Couture at Lewiston, Maine, in September 1946.

Walton was still adjusting his gum shield when Couture punched him on the jaw, knocking him to the canvas, where he lay, out cold.

Count me in

Few boxers can claim they have been on the canvas for more than ten seconds and have still been able to continue fighting. On 22 September 1927 in Chicago, Jack Dempsey lost to Gene Tunney, who retained his world heavyweight title, after a controversial incident occurred.

Dempsey knocked Tunney to the canvas, but the referee, Dave Barry, would not begin the count until Dempsey had retreated to a neutral corner. He eventually had to usher him there, which extended the time the prone Tunney could remain on the canvas.

He was allowed to continue, despite having lain on the canvas for fourteen seconds before the count reached nine. He recovered enough to win on points, thus retaining his title.

The fight has since become known as the Battle of the Long Count.

Self-defeat (1)

Poor Daniel Caruso thought he was performing the perfect warm-up when he began pounding his gloves into his own face before the introductions in the New York Golden Gloves Championships in January 1992.

Although it was a simple psyching-up exercise, Dan was somewhat overenthusiastic in his preparation. He ended up punching himself hard on the nose, breaking and bloodying it, and doctors decided he was unfit to fight.

Self-defeat (2)

During a regional heat of the Saginaw Golden Gloves
Championships in Michigan in 1977, Harvey Gartley
and Dennis Outlette were advised by their teams to be
cautious on their boxing debut: avoid throwing any wild
punches, size up their man for a while, take it slowly.

Forty-seven seconds into the fight, neither man had
managed to land a punch, so the crowd began to grow
restless. Gartley sensed the crowd's impatience, forgot
his orders and panicked, launching a swing towards
Outlette. Unfortunately, he failed to make contact with
his opponent, and the energy with which he had thrown
himself into the punch simply caused him to collapse on
to the canvas and be counted out.

Bobby's fall to fame

A sure-fire way of slipping up in the world of sport is to
disagree with those who sit – or stand – in judgement.
Bobby Frankham, a light-heavyweight, refused to accept
the decision of referee Richie Davies to stop his fight
with Billy Sims of Hackney in the first round at
Wembley in December 1987.

He was so much in disagreement with Davies that he
made him his next opponent, and swung punches at
him. Having twice hit the referee in the face, he decided
to target Sims's corner men, and then start an unofficial
second round with Sims himself.

It was then the rival fans' turn, with the
result that the referee needed a police escort
to accompany him from the ring. The British
Boxing Board of Control said it was an
'utterly disgraceful' episode, and Frankham
said, 'I just had a brainstorm,' adding that it
was 'a bad way to get famous'.

Pre-fight fight

Boxers are particularly sensitive about their 'manhood', it seems, but this curious notion led to a fight *before* the fight in 1994, when the WBO champion Michael Bentt and his challenger Herbie Hide from Norwich brawled at a photocall.

A woman had put a Millwall baseball cap on Bentt's head, but Hide knocked it off and said, 'I want a Norwich cap.' Bentt then hit him in the head and within seconds they were aiming punches at each other while officials and handlers tried to intervene and bring peace to the proceedings.

Both men were judged equally to blame by the British Boxing Board of Control and were each fined £10,000. Bentt said of the fine, 'You don't get anything for fighting outside the ring, but he compromised my manhood.'

Ref put his foot in it

After a fight against Liverpool's Nel Tarleton, in which he was defending his British featherweight title at Anfield in October 1931, Sheffield's Johnny Cuthbert moaned, 'Losing the title was bad enough, but it didn't half rub it in when I realized I'd been beaten by a bloke with one lung and only one foot!'

Things began to go wrong when the referee, while going in to break the men up, trod heavily on Tarleton's foot, causing him considerable pain. The foot continued to throb for the next five rounds, as the Liverpool man hobbled around the ring and the Sheffielder tried to take advantage.

Tarleton was not only challenged mobility-wise, but he also had only one lung, and yet he still managed to win the match on points.

Farr far away

One of the best-known names in British boxing in the 1930s was Welshman Tommy Farr, who became the British heavyweight champion.

In 1933, when he was still nineteen, Farr fought Eddie Steele of Norwood at Crystal Palace, having been called up as a last-minute replacement.

All was going well for Farr, until Steele jabbed him in the throat. The punch had a bizarre effect on the young Welshman, who bolted from the ring and fled to the dressing room. Even years later he would not account for this unusual behaviour.

The disappearing ref

Tom Sayers of Brighton and John C. Heenan of the United States had met for a bare-knuckle fight at Farnborough in Kent on 17 April 1860, and had battled with each other for two hours (thirty-seven hard rounds) when it looked as though Sayers was facing defeat.

However, one of his supporters in the crowd had the bright idea of cutting the ropes to cause the match to be abandoned. Police and spectators spilled into the ring and there was mayhem. Eventually, the situation was brought to order, but during the choas the referee had disappeared. He remained absent for another five rounds, during which the two men fought on without him.

When he did return, he declared the match a draw.

Crowd trouble

Sometimes it is the spectators who are responsible for the sporting screw-up, and never more so than in August 1815 during a bare-knuckle fight on Blackheath, London, between London's Caleb Baldwin, a former England champion, and an Irishman, Bill Ryan.

In what was to be his last bout, Baldwin was exhausted by the twenty-sixth round and slumped to the ground. But Ryan hit him while he was on his knees to cries of 'Foul!' by Baldwin's supporters.

A free-for-all ensued among the crowd, and the Dragoon Guards had to be called to calm things down. By this time, however, the ring had been wrecked and the contest was declared a draw.

And in the tight corner . . .

Occasionally the weather contributes to the sporting slip-up, as in the case of the 1988 European bantamweight match between the reigning champion, Vincenzo Belcastro of Italy, and Britain's Billy Hardy.

The bout had been due to take place in a large marquee that had been erected in Fuscaldo, southern Italy, the champion's home town. Unfortunately, the marquee was wrecked by a gusty wind, so the contest had to be transferred to a sports hall in nearby Paola.

The venue was so inadequate that the spectators were packed in like sardines, leading one sportswriter to comment, 'The only people seated comfortably were the fighters.'

Belcastro won by a small margin.

Down, but not out

It is hard to believe, but even after knocking out an opponent it is still possible to lose a fight, as Joe Lazarus, the US bantamweight, proved in the 1924 Paris Olympics.

Oscar Andren of Sweden was being revived after he had been knocked down and counted out, only to learn that he had won the match. Lazarus, apparently, had been hitting Andren during a clinch just a few seconds before the knockout, which led to his disqualification.

Swedish team officials, wishing to be seen to be the epitome of fairness, even offered a rematch, so embarrassed were they at seeing their man knocked out and yet winning – but officials said no. Andren was declared the winner.

Tooth and jaw

During a bare-knuckle fight between two English-born fighters in Canada in September 1872, Billy Edwards took on Arthur Chambers in the Lightweight Championship of America title fight at Walpole Island. Although Chambers was being soundly beaten, he conned the referee into giving him the match on account of a foul.

When he came out for the twenty-sixth round he screamed that his opponent had bitten him. When the referee, Bill Tracy, saw the teeth marks on Chambers's face, he had no choice but to declare the incident a foul, and award the match to Chambers.

What Tracy was completely unaware of, however, was that Chambers's second, Tom Allen, had been doing the biting between rounds because he knew that his man would never have won by following the rules.

A weighty decision

Though comfort eating can bring short-term happiness, it was by far the wrong option for a South African lightweight boxer named Thomas Hamilton-Brown at the Berlin Olympics in 1936.

Upset that he had lost a split decision to his opponent, Carlos Lillo of Chile, he decided to cheer himself up with a binge, but it transpired that he had not lost the fight after all, because one of the judges had reversed the scores in error.

When Hamilton-Brown's manager went to tell him the good news, the forlorn fighter had already put on 5 pounds (2.25 kilos) in weight and was over the limit for the next bout, which disqualified him from the competition.

Hair today . . .

When the Argentine bantamweight Arnoldo Pares found that he still exceeded the required weight, something had to come off. Since he was only marginally above the maximum poundage, his team decided to cut off his hair, but it was still not enough, and officials duly protested when he remained a few ounces over the limit. Eventually though, it was discovered that the scales had been wrong all along, and so poor old Pares had lost his lovely locks for nothing.

The Leather and the Willow

Of all the games that people choose to make fun of, cricket must be one of the most commonly lampooned. Imagine the confusion of the imaginary man from Mars who stumbles on to a green field on a sunny afternoon in rural England. Knowing something of the language, he hears talk of a 'maiden over' and 'silly mid-off', then glancing up at the scoreboard, is totally bamboozled and bemused as the game goes on for three, four or five days.

While many countries play cricket and consider it one of their national sports, there is somehow something quintessentially English about it. Not surprisingly, this great sport gives rise to a number of mishaps, blunders and humorous moments, of which a great many are featured here.

Close call

Brian Close was fielding in a match between Gloucestershire and Yorkshire in July 1962, and Gloucestershire's Martin Young was batting. Ray Illingworth bowled, and Young hit it to short leg, where Brian Close took it on the temple, and it bounced to Phil Sharpe, who caught it at first slip.

Close was asked by a worried teammate what would have happened if the ball had hit him right between the eyes. With a touch of nonchalance, Close replied, 'He'd have been caught at cover.'

Empty wicket

Communication breakdowns happen in all sports, but sometimes they are funnier than others.

During a match in South Africa, Bobby Simpson was captaining Australia. With a lead of 450, his team were very much in the driving seat by teatime. During the twenty-minute break, Simpson forgot to tell the opposing captain that he wished to enforce the follow-on. So, after tea, both teams came out to field.

Hard to swallow – but true

SBW is a new situation similar to LBW, but means 'swallow before wicket'. It is a rare event, but two instances of the phenomenon have been recorded in the cricketing annals.

The first occasion was in November 1969, when South Australia's Greg Chappell bowled to John Inverarity of Western Australia. The ball hit a swallow in mid-air, and was deflected on to the stumps. The umpire decided it was a no-ball.

At Trimdon, County Durham in 1994, a similar incident occurred when Chris Thomas's ball hit a swallow in flight and was deflected on to the stumps of the batsman, Joe Hall. The umpires conferred and ruled that the ball was dead. Unfortunately, so was the swallow.

Fiery performance

The scorebook could well have read, 'Run out while fighting fire', as that is what actually happened to Stan Dawson, who was batting at Kalgoorlie in Australia in the 1970s.

A quick delivery was bowled that hit him on his hip pocket which contained a box of matches. In an astonishing fluke, some of the matches ignited.

It was while Stan was leaping around beating down the flames with his hands that his opponents ran him out.

Heading for a catch

The Bishop Auckland professional Ricky Waldren completed a straight drive in a match in July 1995, but did not expect to be caught out in quite such an odd manner.

The ball collided with the head of George Simpson, the umpire at the bowler's end, and was caught by an opposing fielder right out on the boundary.

Simpson went to hospital. Waldren went to the pavilion.

Giving it their best shot

It was the first ball of the match when Bunbury of Western Australia were at home to a touring team from Victoria in the late-nineteenth century. The visiting side's opening batsman banged the ball right into a tree, where it became stuck.

The batsmen began to run . . .

Fielders tried in vain to get the ball out of the tree while the batsmen continued to run.

The next ploy was to look for an axe to fell the tree, but meanwhile the batsmen ran and ran – and ran some more . . .

Finally, somebody produced a rifle, and shot down the offending ball, by which time the batsmen, doubtless shattered after their exertions, had scored 286 runs.

In for a penny?

In his Test debut for England against Australia at Lord's in 1975, David Steele was naturally a bit nervous.

As he set off from the dressing room, bound for the field of play, he descended an extra flight of steps in error and ended up in the pavilion toilets.

Home and away

Entire books are written about cricket tours, but one was not all that it seemed. E. H. D. Sewell's *From a Window at Lord's* describes the MCC's 1936–7 tour to Australia, written as soon as the tour ended. Strangely, though, the author had never left England.

Ian's X file

Not all sporting screw-ups occur on the field of play. Ian Greig, the England cricketer, had to go to hospital for an

X-ray after hurting his hand in a match against Pakistan in 1987, where it was confirmed that he had a fracture in a finger bone.

It was not such a bad break, and he was likely to recover quickly, but as he stood to leave, he banged his head on the X-ray machine, leaving him with a wound needing two stitches.

In for a duck?

It is unlikely that any cricket ground these days can boast a pond. One that could, however, was the ground at Malton, Yorkshire, when the local cricket team was visited by a neighbouring team from Scarborough in 1922.

The pond was just beyond the boundary rope in one corner, and the man batting was a big hitter called Charles Inglis Thornton – the type of batsman able to push fields further and further out.

Thornton was also able to get shots between the fielders, until he hit the ball very close to one of them on the boundary. The unfortunate fellow thought the ball might just clear his head, so he ran backwards, trying to make a catch.

The inevitable happened, of course, and into the pond he fell.

Here come da Judge (quack, quack!)

Many a cricketer has experienced the humiliation of being bowled for a duck. To be bowled for two first-ball ducks in successive balls in the same match is quite an achievement, however, and it happened to the Glamorgan tailender Peter Judge in 1946.

After being the last man out against the Indian tourists at Cardiff Arms Park, he was bowled first ball by the leg

spinner Chandra Sarwate. Time was running out, and
India decided to enforce the follow-on. The Glamorgan
captain Johnnie Clay signalled to Judge to remain in the
middle to start the next innings. The opening bowler was
once again Sarwate, who managed to clean-bowl the
hapless Judge with the first ball.

Into the long grass

It is not only golf balls that disappear into the long grass;
cricket balls do, too.

When Macleod played against Banyale in a Victoria
country match at Windsor Reserve in 1990, Garry
Chapman, the Banyale batsman, hit the ball to mid-
wicket and it went into grass of about 25 centimetres in
height. The batsmen scored seventeen runs while the
fielders searched for it.

It all ended in tears

At a first-class cricket match between England and the
West Indies at Sabina Park in Kingston, Jamaica, things
got out of hand when the crowd became rather annoyed
about the dismissal of one of the West Indian batsmen,
Basil Butcher.

They began to hurl bottles on to the pitch and one hit
the England captain, Colin Cowdrey, on the foot. He
appealed for them to calm down, but his words either
could not be heard or they simply fell on deaf ears.

So the police entered the fray, and sprayed the crowd
with tear gas. Unfortunately, they had not checked the
wind direction first, and so the gas drifted off into the
pavilion. It travelled further than the pavilion too, and
was carried on the wind into the parliament building,
where the Cabinet was in session, forcing a premature
suspension of proceedings.

Just the ticket

Ilfracombe Rugby Club ground at Hele in Devon sits on
a steep hill, which can make life rather difficult for fielders
at times when cricket is played there.

Paul Crabb was playing for the club's cricket section
against a neighbouring team, Woolacombe, in July 1996,
when a ball was hit out of the ground. Crabb chased it,
but it bounced on to a road, and the road was a hill, and
the ball began to roll.

Crabb followed in hot pursuit – 100 yards, 200 yards,
300 yards; eventually, a quarter of a mile away from the
ground, the ball finally came to a halt.

He was about to turn round and run back up the hill to
return to the match, but a bus arrived and when he told
the driver what had happened, the tired fielder was
offered a free ride.

In similar circumstances in 1997, a ball that was hit out
of the ground during a match between schools from
Macclesfield and Bangor landed on a passing lorry and
was never seen again.

Huffing and puffing

Robin Wightman was a bit annoyed when his captain
refused to allow him to bowl the final over. It was an
understandable reaction as Robin, who was playing for

Whiteleas against East Rainton in the North East
Durham League in August 1995, had already taken
seven wickets.

His captain would not back down, so Wightman
stormed off the pitch and would not return.

When Whiteleas went in to bat, Wightman's departure
was recorded in the scorebook as 'absent, huffed'.

Out!

It seems that scorers do not mince words when the
reasons for a cricketer's absence must be accurately
recorded and displayed.

In the case of Abdul Aziz, who was injured in the first
innings of the final of the 1958–9 Qaid-I-
Azam Trophy in Karachi, the scorecard
read, 'Abdul Aziz retired hurt . . . 0'.

The injury proved to be fatal,
however, so the scorer wrote for the
second innings, 'Abdul Aziz did not bat,
dead . . . 0'.

Machine madness

A bowler would doubtless show some compassion if a
batsman was down, despite being on opposing sides; not
so a bowling machine.

It was during the winter of 1985–6 and Martyn
Goulding of Torquay had decided to hone his batting skills
with the help of a bowling machine.

Things were going well until the machine sent a 75-
m.p.h. delivery, which hit Martyn's foot and broke it. But
while he was down on the ground, gripping his foot in
agony, the machine continued its relentless assault, and
down came another fast delivery, which hit him in the
chest and broke two ribs.

The ups and downs of it

At the end of the 1996 Mercantile Mutual Insurance Cup tie with New South Wales in Sydney, South Australia left the field thinking they had lost the fifty-over match by a run, but it was discovered that the scorers had not taken account of a no-ball in the forty-eighth over, and so the two extra runs turned their defeat into a three-wicket victory.

The New South Wales team, by contrast, were less impressed with their short-lived triumph.

No-ball!

An important piece of equipment was missing when Derbyshire and Shropshire were poised to do battle in a NatWest Trophy match at Chesterfield in June 1990.

Someone had forgotten to bring the match balls, so a new batch had to be sent for from county headquarters in Derby, delaying the start of the match by forty-five minutes.

On me 'ead, sun

England's all-rounder Chris Lewis decided on a new image for the 1993–4 tour of the West Indies. Whether it was for reasons of vanity or in an effort to keep himself cool, he decided to shave his head completely, transforming his appearance.

Unfortunately, though, he forgot to wear his hat and got sunstroke.

Pockets and sockets

The World Series match at Colombo between Sri Lanka and Zimbabwe in 1996 had to be delayed for eight minutes because no one could find the bails. They were eventually located in the groundsman's pocket.

In 1975, one of the rarest events in cricket occurred at a County Championship match between Leicestershire and Lancashire. The Leicestershire wicketkeeper, Barry Dudleston, stumped the Lancashire batsman, David Lloyd, but the bails leaped up off the stumps and landed right back in position in their sockets. Lloyd took full advantage of this extraordinary reprieve, and went on to make a century.

Strictly for the Bird

When Dickie Bird was overseeing a match at Northampton, Allan Lamb came in to bat and handed his mobile phone to the famous umpire, saying, 'Look after this for me, please, Dickie. I didn't want to leave it in the dressing room.'

After about five minutes' play, Lamb's phone began chirping and Bird, realizing it was not a small feathered creature that was making the noise, had no alternative but to answer it. To his bemusement, Ian Botham was at the end of the line, calling to ask for the score.

For Dickie Bird, this was not the first time technology had distracted him from the more sedate sound of willow on leather. On one occasion at Bournemouth, during his playing days with Yorkshire, he was due to face a ball against Hampshire when his attention was diverted. He was sure he could hear the frenetic tones of a racing commentary, and he noticed that over in the slips Colin Ingleby-Mackenzie had a transistor radio pressed to his ear.

'Hope I'm not breaking your concentration, old chap,' the fielder called out. 'I've got a few bob riding on a nag.'

Pyrrhic victory

It was a long way to the boundary for David O'Sullivan, who was fielding for New Zealand in the First Test of the 1973–4 series in Australia. Off he went in pursuit of a rolling ball, hoping to reach it before it went over the boundary for a four.

After a full-length dive, he stopped the ball just before it rolled over the rope. However, in the time it had taken him to get to the boundary, do the dive, pick up the ball and throw it, the batsmen had made five runs.

Rain stopped, play began

When rain stopped play on the last day of the County Championship match between Hampshire and Glamorgan in June 1969, there were two hours left at the Bournemouth ground, and an early finish to the match looked inevitable.

So the Hampshire players left the ground to return to their respective homes, as the match, as far as they knew, had been abandoned. The rain stopped, however, and play was due to resume, or it would have done had the Hampshire team returned.

Glamorgan's men entered the field and remained for the regulation two minutes before being awarded a win by the umpires.

All was not lost, however. The MCC, which arbitrates in such matters, decided the Hampshire side were victims of a misunderstanding, and rescinded the umpires' decision.

Reined in by rain

Sidney Wells had been looking forward to this day. At last, in 1927, he was selected for his first – and only – first-class match. It was against Kent.

The British weather got the better of the occasion, though, and the match was deluged. Not a ball was bowled. Poor Sid was out of first-class cricket before he had even got in.

Too, too bad

South Africa's top Anglican cleric, Archbishop Desmond Tutu, wanted to visit the dressing room at tea on the first day of the First Test at Lord's in July 1994, when his country's team was making its first appearance in England for twenty-nine years.

He had not counted on the strict attitude of the Lord's stewards, however, who stopped him from entering the pavilion because he was not wearing a jacket.

Revolutionary!

It was to be the first overseas cricket tour. The date was August 1789, the year of the French Revolution. The England team were about to go to Paris for a fixture organized by the Duke of Dorset, a major player in the cricketing world of the time, and also the British ambassador in Paris at the start of the Revolution.

The team travelled to Dover ready for the Channel crossing, having been told they would have safe passage, in spite of the troubles. However, before they could embark, they saw none other than the Duke himself, fleeing Paris.

In the interests of safety, a decision was taken to abandon the match.

Ribbet, ribbet!

It was a strange old wicket for the final Test during England's tour of South Africa in 1922–3. The ball stopped almost dead after it had been pitched on the Durban ground.

When batsmen tentatively prodded the wicket they did not find a natural irregularity such as a bump in the ground, but a pile of small green frogs.

Play was suspended so that the creatures could be removed for their own safety.

Setting an example

At a match in the early 1960s, Jon Fellows-Smith, the South African captain of Northamptonshire, was adamant that the wet wicket was perfectly safe to play on. However, his pace men were a bit reluctant to open the bowling. The pitch, they claimed, was just too dangerous.

Fellows-Smith decided to set an example to his players by opening the bowling himself, but slipped on his run-up and had to be taken to hospital with a broken ankle.

The spilling fields

In the 1975–6 Test series between the West Indies and India, Clive Lloyd made 70 in the Second Test, allowing the West Indies to achieve a draw, and ultimately gain a 2–1 series win against India.

However, Lloyd would not have made such a score had it not been for the enthusiasm of two fielders as he sent the ball towards mid-off. Eknath Solkar and Brijesh Patel went to catch it at the same time neither, it seems, aware of the other's presence. The mid-air collision was inevitable, and the ball landed on the grass, leaving Lloyd still at the crease.

To cap it all . . .

M. J. K. Smith was about to take a ball from Hampshire bowler Malcolm Heath at Edgbaston in May 1962, when a gust of wind took his cap off and it landed on the wicket. The former Warwickshire and England captain was given out, 'hit wicket'.

Tooth decay

In April 1997, while groundsman Brian Lucas was rolling the hallowed turf at the Perkins Cricket Club in Shropshire, he sneezed and his false teeth shot out.

Unable to stop the machine in time, the roller went over the prized dentures, and crushed them beyond recognition, leaving Lucas sans teeth.

Yes! By that I mean no!

Should we? Shouldn't we? It can sometimes be a difficult decision whether to make the run or stay put. Godfrey Evans, an England wicketkeeper, made an entertaining run during the Third Test against Australia at Sydney in the 1950–1 Ashes series.

Evans set off to run, but got Doug Wright run out after sending him back and then changing his mind.

This stop-go performance eventually cost England the game by an innings and thirteen runs, because poor old Wright, in trying to respond to his colleague's equivocation, pulled a groin muscle that put paid to his bowling for the rest of the match.

You must be choking!

Australia had declared on 729 for 6, leaving England facing a first-innings deficit of 304 in the Second Test at Lord's in 1930.

Percy Chapman had reached 121 when a bluebottle flew into his mouth, causing him to choke. Coughing madly, he was caught behind, not having added to his score. Australia went on to win by seven wickets.

Sheep stop play

In Ebbw Vale, in 1948, Glamorgan's county match against Gloucestershire was progressing nicely until play had to be stopped when a flock of sheep decided that the grass on the cricket field was better than their usual grazing area.

Sheep are not the only animals to halt a match. Only nine months before the incident in Wales, South Australia were playing Queensland when the game was stopped after thousands of grasshoppers landed on the pitch.

In 1962 a swarm of bees were unwelcome visitors at the Parks, during a match between Oxford University and Worcestershire.

Players get the hump

Animals of a more exotic nature have also been known to put a stop to cricket matches. In the match between Launceston and Old Suttonians in August 1984, play had to be stopped on four occasions because a herd of camels wandered on to the pitch; they had strayed from a nearby circus.

A shattering experience

In 1985 at Holton-Le-Clay, Dennis Lovesey, who lived near the local cricket ground, had grown so tired of spectators' cars blocking access to his house, he drove his lorry on to the pitch and parked it right in the middle, refusing to move it.

Eventually, officials prevailed upon him to move the vehicle after they had appealed to the offending drivers to stop blocking Mr Lovesey's drive.

According to a report in the cricketer's bible, *Wisden*, a similar incident occurred eight years later. A lorry driver was so enraged after a six had flown out of the cricket ground at Wansford, near Peterborough, and shattered his windscreen, that he parked his lorry on the pitch. He would not move until insurance details had been exchanged.

A smashing six

Cricket balls have been known to go through car windows, especially at small grounds where players' and spectators' cars may well be within a well-batted six of the crease. But the impact of the ball bowled by Walsden cricketer Peter Green, had a more personal touch.

When he delivered the ball to Rochdale's Wilson Hartley in a Central Lancashire League match, Hartley whacked the ball with his accustomed gusto and off it went for a soaring six, right into an adjoining street and through the window of a house – Peter Green's house.

Bowled out of a decent benefit

Sometimes it does not pay to be too good at one's job. Bertie Buse was a Somerset all-rounder whose benefit match at Bath took place against Lancashire in June 1953. The pitch was rather perky and so after the Somerset team had been bowled out for only fifty-five runs, Buse decided to put his fiery bowling into action.

He took six wickets and Lancashire were bowled out for 158. Somerset came in again, but fared little better and were out for seventy-nine runs, leaving Lancashire the winners by an innings and twenty-four runs.

Ironically, it was Buse's bowling prowess that contributed to the end of the match on the first day, which severely reduced the revenue for Buse's own benefit match.

A costly drop

In June 1994, players and spectators at the Warwickshire v Durham game at Edgbaston witnessed one of the costliest dropped catches of all time. Warwickshire's Brian Lara had made just eighteen runs, and sent what appeared to be a simple catch to the Durham wicketkeeper, Chris Scott. Lara realized his error and had started his walk back to the pavilion, but Scott dropped it.

Feeling thoroughly infuriated with himself, the wicketkeeper sighed, 'I suppose he'll go on and get a century now.' How wrong he was, for Lara went on to make not one century but five, finishing on 501 not out.

It's just not cricket!

Thomas White of Reigate in Surrey was bowled out quite often and, understandably, did not appreciate it. One day in September 1771 he turned up for a game between the Chertsey club and Hambledon with a cricket bat that was much wider than the wicket.

There are rules to prevent such activity now, but in 1771, Mr White's opponents were left completely stumped.

Written off

Former England all-rounder Derek Pringle did not sustain his back injury after twisting awkwardly to catch the ball while dashing towards the boundary.

When sitting down while writing a letter, Pringle leaned back in his chair and – ouch! – damaged his back.

Clapped out

A popular player, the West Indian cricketer Clive Lloyd received a great many ovations. His fans were particularly appreciative on the occasion of his last game, which was held at Lord's.

So they clapped, and then clapped some more. And then they stood and turned it into a standing ovation.

Unfortunately, hardly had their hands stopped smarting from the welcome, than they were clapping again, as Lloyd returned to the pavilion – out for a duck.

A wee indiscretion

It is impossible to ignore the call of nature; you just have to go, but not on a cricket pitch, in front of a multitude of spectators.

In 1995 Wayne Radcliffe of the Yorkshire club Newmillerdam fell foul of a ruling made by the Wakefield and District Cricket Union, which banned him for five years for urinating on the pitch. Radcliffe had to plead guilty, but in mitigation he said he had been desperate and, anyway, had turned towards some trees to prevent spectators from witnessing the act and to protect his modesty.

Bare facts

Streakers are so familiar on sports fields these days that spectators barely raise an eyebrow. But a couple of streakers who attempted to get their fifteen seconds of fame during the Asia–Rest of the World game at the Oval rather wished they had thought better of it and stayed fully clothed. Ultimately they were chased and dealt with by what one journalist writing of the incident described as, 'those lovely Oval stewards who are better suited to belonging to the SAS than showing people where to sit'.

Blowing their cover

During the 1996 World Cup between Kenya and Zimbabwe in Lahore, a helicopter was used to dry the pitch with its powerful downdraught after rain had stopped play.

But all it managed to do was to blow the covers away, spilling even more water on to the pitch. As a consequence the match was abandoned altogether.

A Case of severe nerves

Somerset's Cecil Case was a bag of nerves after he had been given out 'hit wicket' in a match against Nottinghamshire at Taunton in 1932. He had fallen on the stumps while trying to avoid being hit by a rather lively ball from Bill Voce.

In fact, Case was so nervous that, instead of picking up his bat to take back to the pavilion, he marched back with one of the stumps under his arm.

On Fairway and Green

The game of golf has produced countless amusing moments at the expense of players and spectators alike. From lost balls and wayward caddies to over-zealous fans and baffling bunkers, the life of a golfer is never dull, and often beset by a catalogue of mishaps and mistakes.

King, Clark and a cow
Cows eat grass and the odd bramble, sometimes even the odd nettle, but gutta-percha?

It happened in 1963 as S. C. King played R. W. Clark on the tenth hole at Guernsey. Clark had hit his shot into the rough, and while looking for his ball, he found that a cow was eating it.

The pair played the course again the next day, but but decided to keep a close eye out for bovine intruders. This time it was King whose ball landed in the rough, while Clark's was safe on the fairway.

Remembering the cow incident, Clark put his hat over the ball, and went off into the rough to help his opponent to find his wayward shot. But when he returned to the fairway the cow was there again, and this time she had eaten his hat.

Jaws – the game!

In Britain, the only animal you are likely to see as you drive your ball down the fairway is the odd rabbit or squirrel, dog or cat. It would be somewhat of a shock to read a sign saying 'Do not feed the alligators', therefore, an example of which can be found at the Marriott Hotel golf course in Orlando, Florida.

However, on the third hole in the third round of the Zimbabwe Open at Harare in 1993, Ben Fouchee and Jurie Visagie, both South Africans, almost had a close encounter of the snappy kind with the course crocodile.

As he crossed a bridge, Visagie nearly trod on the crocodile's tail, which could have had catastrophic results. He finished with an 80 and said he was lucky to be alive. Fouchee finished on 71, but put that down to the fact that the same crocodile went for his wife, who was caddying for him, leaving him to concentrate on his shots.

Making a breast of it

In 1994 Tony Jacklin was trying to get out of a bunker on the thirteenth hole during a British Seniors event. In his attempt to lift the ball clear of the bunker, it rebounded on to his chest. Unaware that there was a penalty for this type of incident, he put the wrong score on his card. As a result he was disqualified.

Off the ball

Missing the hole is one thing, but missing the ball is another matter entirely. It does happen, as Hale Irwin proved in the third round of the 1983 Open at Royal Birkdale.

He had left his putt no more than a couple of centimetres from the hole on the par-3 fourteenth, and must have taken his eyes off the ball as he went to tap it in, for he missed hitting it completely.

Irwin incurred a one-stroke penalty, which cost him the match. He ended up as joint second, one stroke behind the winner, Tom Watson.

One too many

The Welsh golfer Ian Woosnam managed to lose £218,334 in winnings, and all because he was carrying one club too many.

At the 2001 Open at Royal Lytham and St Anne's, Woosnam was docked two strokes for carrying fifteen clubs instead of fourteen. He had just birdied the first and had gone back into the joint lead, when his caddie, Miles Byrne, told him that he was carrying an extra driver. Woosnam finished the tournament joint third, four strokes behind the winner, David Duval, but without the two-stroke penalty he would have been runner-up, and considerably richer.

Presidential problems

Presidents Bill Clinton, George Bush Sr and Gerald Ford were enjoying a game of golf in the Bob Hope Invitation Tournament at Indian Wells in California when, on the first hole, Bush sent a spirited drive right between the eyes of a San Diego woman, shattering her glasses. She was given first aid and taken to the Eisenhower Medical Center for ten stitches.

Later on, Bush still had another target to hit: on the fourteenth he pelted a spectator on the buttock.

Ford caused similar spectator damage during the tournament: while playing the seventeenth he hit a woman on the finger, drawing blood.

Snakes alive!

The moral of this tale is, be careful when you reprimand your caddie, because his reaction may be rather extreme. This might have been the case at the 1985 South African Masters, where Vaughan Tucker gave a caddie a ticking off because he had moved the player's ball without permission.

But the caddie was not happy to be spoken to so harshly, and disappeared into the rough for a while, returning a moment later with a snake in his hand, which he proceeded to shake at the terrified Tucker.

Photo finish

If victory in a major championship is virtually assured, a golfer would doubtless have no objections to seeing the press there to record his outstanding achievement. In 1937 Harold McSpaden did not share this view, however, when Densmore Shute retained his US PGA title as a result of McSpaden's bad luck.

McSpaden had a 1.2-metre (4-foot) putt for victory at the last hole, but the snapping photographers disturbed his concentration. He missed the putt and lost the first extra hole.

A most expensive putt

When is a piece of sand not a piece of sand? When it's a piece of grass, of course, and it loses you the Open.

At St Andrews in 1970, Doug Sanders needed to cover about 30 feet to beat the great Jack Nicklaus. He had to do it in two putts, but his first left him 30 inches short of the hole.

'I was confident, standing over it, and then I saw what I thought was a little piece of sand on my line,' Sanders told reporters afterwards. 'Without moving my feet, I bent down to pick it up, but it was a piece of grass. I didn't take time to move away and get reorganized. I mishit the ball and pushed it to the right of the hole. It was the most expensive missed putt in the history of the game.'

The following day he lost the eighteen-hole play-off to Nicklaus by a single stroke.

Cooper's blooper

Henry Cooper, better known as a boxer than a golfer, was nonetheless fond of a round or two of golf.

On one occasion his trousers split, right in the wrong place. 'I didn't have a clue what to do,' Cooper told reporters. 'But about thirty women around the green rushed forward offering safety pins.'

Having a ball - or not

To lose one ball may be regarded as a misfortune. To lose seven looks like carelessness. But Sweden's Anders Forsbrand managed to do just that after taking ninety-three shots for seventeen holes in the 1994 French Open at the national course in Paris. He ran out of balls on the eighteenth.

He had lost five in water and another pair had gone into some deep rough.

Having a splashing time

Generally, it is nice to have fans, and Gary Player must have thought so too when he came off the eighteenth green at the Congressional Country Club after a practice round in 1976.

Finding himself besieged by autograph hunters, Player reached for his pen. But the fans were so eager that they pushed him into a lake.

A wee question of priorities

The moral of this story: when caddying in an important match, make sure you visit the loo before stepping out on to the course.

The American caddie Chuck Hoersch did not, and it cost his boss, Sophie Gustafson, the £110,000 first prize in the WPGA International match at Gleneagles in 2001.

Gustafson was playing Laura Davies in the semi-finals, and finished all square. But in the following play-off, Hoersch decided he could not wait any longer, and nipped to the portaloo. Then, to catch up with the action, he used a buggy.

However, the rules state that caddies as well as players must walk, not ride, and so Gustafson was disqualified. But for the fact that Gustafson is his girlfriend, Hoersch may well have found himself an ex-employee after such a costly mistake.

Crazy golf

Golfing etiquette was all but forgotten in a game in 1993 at Sabal Palm Golf Club in Florida. Two players, Howard Polley and John Tennyson, were aggrieved by the fact that another player, Hugo Torres, and his fellows were too slow.

To show their contempt, Tennyson and Polley played the seventh without even nodding to Torres and his party, or in any way acknowledging their presence. Their behaviour upset Torres to such an extent that an argument developed and Torres hit Tennyson across the back with his pitching wedge, while Polley then took a swing at Torres. At this point Torres's arm got in the way, and the club broke. In spite of the pain he was suffering, Torres summoned up enough energy to stab Polley in the neck with the broken shaft of his own club, and Tennyson and Polley ended up in hospital. Torres was obliged to pay a visit to the local jail, where he was released on $10,000 bail.

They never did finish their game.

Horns of a dilemma

During a game between Otway Hayes of South Africa and John Panton of the United Kingdom at Houghton Golf Club in Johannesburg in 1951, a woman golfer wearing a bright red sweater became the focus of some very unwanted attention.

There was a scream. The players looked up to see a bull in full charge, horns lowered, heading towards the hapless damsel in distress. Fortunately, she was quick-witted enough first to hide behind a tree, and then to don a mackintosh to cover the offending sweater. The bull, no longer able to see the rage-making stimulus, just sauntered off.

Dark deed

Sports injuries are all part of the job, an occupational hazard, they come with the territory. But sustaining a more mundane injury away from the sportsfield is somewhat less acceptable.

During the Ryder Cup in the United States in 1971, the American Billy Casper had to miss the singles match because of a broken toe. He had damaged the digit while groping around in his St Louis hotel in the dark, trying to find his bedroom.

Bunkered!

Within the context of golf, being rescued from the bunker usually means getting your ball out and back on to the fairway. Not so for D. J. Bayley MacArthur, playing at Rose Bay, New South Wales, in 1931.

His ball landed in a dreaded bunker and naturally he went in to retrieve it, but in seconds he found himself up to his armpits in sand, so heavy had been the rain.

The 89-kilogram (14-stone) MacArthur shouted for help which, thankfully, arrived.

Caught with his pants up

If he had not been at such pains to keep his trousers clean, Craig Stadler might have been joint second in the 1987 San Diego Open at Torrey Pines. He had hit a shot that had gone underneath a bush, and the position of the ball was so awkward that it was necessary for Stadler to kneel to get to it.

He was rather too fond of his trousers, though, and to muddy them by kneeling was more than he could stand. So he knelt on a small towel that his caddie used to clean his golf balls. This was strictly against the rules, however, because it constituted 'building a stance'. His misdemeanour had not passed unnoticed, either, because the match was televised, and some viewers phoned in the following day. As a result, Stadler was disqualified for not having included the penalty in the score he had signed for the previous day.

Aiming for the cup (1)

Golf balls land in strange places, but Hale Irwin, taking part in a 1973 United States tour event, did not expect his to land where it did – within the bra of a spectator.

Fortunately, he was spared the embarrassment of

removing the ball from its resting place with the club of his choice; instead he allowed the woman to remove it herself.

Aiming for the cup (2)

Great Britain's Leonard Crawley may not have been aiming for the cup exactly, but the result was the same. It was during the 1932 Walker Cup match at Brooklyn, when Crawley's wayward drive to the eighteenth managed to hit the treasured trophy, on display outside the clubhouse, giving it a severe dent.

Thrills on Wheels

There's nothing quite like the noise and the smell of the race track. Exhaust fumes fill the air as the whine of engines provides the incidental music to one of the most thrilling sports on earth. However, this high-powered sport is certainly not without its tales of craziness, stupidity and downright doziness.

The wrong formula

Some people, it seems, are fated not to make it. Bobby Unser was a legend in the Indy 500. He had won it on three occasions – 1968, 1975 and 1981 – but, when he attempted to compete in Formula One with BRM, luck was not on his side.

In 1968, the year he first won the Indy, he wanted to race in the Italian Grand Prix, but a prior commitment in the United States caused him to pull out. Then, at Watkins Glen, New York, he crashed a car while practising, and managed to blow a couple of engines, too. So he took a different car for the race itself, but had to retire with engine failure, and it proved to be his one and only attempt at Formula One racing.

Hop in, love

The British driver Tony Fall had stopped his Lancia to wait for the correct time at the final control in the 1969 Portuguese TAP Rally, and was greeted by his wife.

As the crowd surged forward, the police asked if he could drive on towards the control. Obligingly, Fall told his wife to jump aboard while he moved the car the 10 metres or so to reach the control. Technically, though, he was carrying an unauthorized passenger when he was crossing the finishing line, and was duly disqualified.

Seconds away

Poor George Grinton did not appreciate the difference between minutes and seconds when, during the 1925 sidecar Tourist Trophy on the Isle of Man, he got a signal from the pit saying '3'.

Grinton mistakenly believed he was three minutes ahead of the rest of the field. He decided to slow down a little, to avoid taking unnecessary risks, believing himself to be in an unassailable position. As two cars suddenly came into view, and raced past him at high speed, he soon realized that the signal actually meant three seconds, not three minutes.

Sure enough, a somewhat crestfallen Grinton ended up third.

Vintage comedy

They had to let the train take the strain back in 1896 on

the occasion of the first London-to-Brighton Rally.

Only fourteen out of the thirty entrants reached Brighton by road. During the run, a Bollée tricycle managed to nip through a hedge and was towed out by a cart. Another machine turned turtle, and ended up – complete with occupants – in a pond.

And others that were unable to make it under their own steam had to be taken to the south coast by train.

The chequered rag

For some inexplicable and rather infuriating reason, Rudolf Caracciola's leading Mercedes began to slow down quite dramatically as he neared the finish in the 1937 British Grand Prix at Donington.

The cause of his failure to cross the line first became apparent when, having finished third, he looked over his car and found that an oily rag had been left by one of his mechanics in the supercharger.

My giddy ant(eater)

Imagining the many different types of obstacles that could get in one's way is a racing driver's nightmare; hitting any sort of object at such high speed can be damaging and devastating, and change the course of a race.

During the 1963 East African Safari Rally, Swedish driver Erik Carlsson was leading the event in his Saab when he hit an anteater.

Putting his foot under it

Track marshals managed to hamper the progress of René Arnoux when his Ferrari stopped with an electrical fault.

On the occasion of the 1983 South African Grand Prix

at Kyalami, Arnoux was in the middle of a qualifying session. His car stationary, he asked the marshals if they could push it to a safer place. They did – but went over Arnoux's foot, leaving it badly swollen for the race.

Size does count
Nigel Mansell had been signed up for McLaren for just two months, but had to withdraw from the opening two races of the 1995 Formula One World Championship because the cockpit in the McLaren Mercedes was too small. He had to be replaced by Mark Blundell, who slotted into the cockpit cosily.

Size counted in a different way when Peter Harper's Sunbeam Tiger was disqualified from the Coupe des Alpes in 1966 – he had an exhaust that was too small. Not too large, which would have given him an advantage, but too small, which could not have given him any extra power.

Fall guy
While waving to the crowd after finishing fourth in the 500cc US Motor Cycle Championship in 1989, Kevin Magee fell off his bike and broke his leg.

As you were

Louis Chrion of France had been taking part in the
Monte Carlo Rally during the 1920s when he found
himself, and his car, in a ditch. It took hours for him to
get the car out of the ditch and back on the road, only to
be shunted back into the ditch by another competitor.

On his head be it

Mika Hakkinen's team boss, Ron Dennis, was not too
pleased with his driver when Hakkinen drove out of the
McLaren garage to get to the starting grid for the 1999
Australian Grand Prix in Melbourne.

Hakkinen was unaware that his air line was still attached
to his car, which pulled down a gantry – right on to Ron
Dennis's head.

Dastardly and Muttley, eat your hearts out!

Winning is all, and some people will go to extraordinary
lengths to achieve victory, which is what happened
during the 1902 Paris–Vienna road race.

For Charles Jarrott, driving a Panhard, the trouble
began when, on the second day, the car's wooden chassis
collapsed as it approached the overnight stop at
Bregenz. Jarrott, though, was determined not to let a few
pieces of wood get in the way of success. All that was
needed was some way to strengthen the frame, and they
could at least make it to the end of the next stage, which
was at Salzburg.

Still pondering on the problem of how to repair the
chassis, Jarrott and his trusty mechanic George Du Cros
retired for the night at their hotel in Bregenz. Then
Jarrott had an idea, which he explained later: 'I was just
getting into bed and had turned to put out the light,

when my eye fell upon a stand used for carrying a tray,' he said. 'And in a second I perceived that the four legs of that stand were exactly what I wanted.'

It was a bit late to ask the proprietor if they could buy the stand, so they decided to take it and answer questions later.

Then came *le deuxième problème*: how to drill holes in these suddenly priceless pieces of wood, to accommodate the bolts. Du Cros suggested it would be a good idea to drill against the wall in order to get better purchase. Jarrott was to recall, 'He was delightfully successful, but the trouble was that he drove it through too far and brought down half the plaster. And then, in endeavouring to show how easy it was on another portion of the wall, he succeeded in bringing that down, also.'

But their problems did not end there, as Jarrott managed to bore a hole in his arm and, in an effort to staunch the bleeding, ripped up bed sheets to use as a bandage.

Jarrott recalled, 'There was nothing in the room we did not utilize for something or other. I hate to think what must have been the expression on the proprietor's face when he discovered what had taken place.'

The next problem was how to get the pieces of wood out of the hotel without being discovered. The solution they reached was to put them down their trouser legs.

This is what they did, and they managed to repair the vehicle and get it back on the road. They eventually reached Salzburg and carried on towards Vienna. Problems were still arising at every turn for, at one point, Du Cros had to lie on the bonnet and hold a towel against the pipe to keep the water in the radiator.

Less than four miles from Vienna, the Panhard's gearbox broke. Jarrott 'borrowed' a bicycle and rode for help. But Du Cros could not just sit idle so, while Jarrott was away, he managed to obtain help from a horse-drawn cab. When Jarrott got back, he saw the car being towed behind the cab to the finishing line, and was aghast.

An indignant Jarrott cut the tow rope and got behind the Panhard's wheel, managing to guide the spluttering car across the finish line. And the engine finally went phutt-phutt, and died.

Fire and water

For reasons unknown, no one told Franco Cortese that his treasured Alfa Romeo had gone up in flames on the eve of the 1933 Mille Miglia. An electric spark had ignited some petrol fumes, and the car was no more than a burned-out shell.

Cortese only discovered the distressing situation four hours before the start. Immediately he set about overseeing the rebuilding of the car and, with just an hour to go before the start, all had gone well and Cortese looked like he had a functional car in which to race. However, one of the mechanics had contrived to pour water, instead of petrol, into the fuel tank, which then had to be removed and cleaned out.

Cortese was late for the start of the race and, although he expected to win, he came in second.

Twenty-one years later in the same race, just after the start, Giuseppe Farina hit a tree while trying to avoid a spectator who had strayed on to the road. Farina, in a Ferrari, was out of racing for two months after suffering a broken arm.

In 1957, the same race witnessed a spectacular crash after the French daredevil Jean Behra decided to do some last-minute practice before the race. He was hospitalized after his Maserati had crashed into a lorry.

Back in 1932, an unfortunate collision took place

between Nazio Nuvolari's Ferrari Alfa Romeo and a tree. Nuvolari's co-driver was Gianbattista Guidotti, who was given quite a fright by men in cloaks. When he came round at the side of the road, he could not see Nuvolari, but realized he was on a stretcher that was being carried by four men wearing what he thought were Ku Klux Klan robes. So he shut his eyes and pretended to be dead.

Fortunately, the mysterious figures were just monks from a local order, who traditionally helped drivers injured in the Mille Miglia. They were merely taking him to their monastery hospital for treatment.

Crew cut

Raymond Joss had no time to lose during the 1963 Monte Carlo Rally. He and his crew of three were on the Chartreuse special stage, when their Rover three-litre car went off the road.

Two crew members got out to push the car back on the road but, impatient to get going again, he sped off, leaving one of his crew in the road; he had been unable to get back into the car in time. The hapless crew member went to drink some wine with locals in a bakery and watch as the other competitors sped by.

Ultimately, Joss's impatience proved to be his downfall: for crossing the line without a full complement of crew, he was disqualified.

Snow fun

Spectators can often be a liability when a rally championship is at stake.

During Stage 3 of the Monte Carlo Rally in 1994, the even leader Armin Schwarz and second-placed Colin McRae both skidded on snow thrown by spectators, and left the road. Schwarz ended up in overall seventh place, while McRae was tenth.

In the 1968 Monte Carlo Rally, drunken spectators threw snow on to the road during a tricky mountain section, while Gerard Larrousse was vying for the lead in a works Renault Alpine.

Information that is the pits

It was the final hour of the 1935 Le Mans 24-Hour Race when René-Louis Dreyfus's Alfa Romeo caught up with a Lagonda, believed to be the leading car, which looked to be in a rather bad state, having had to make several stops due to oil-pressure problems.

So when Dreyfus's pit colleagues said he had passed the leading car, he felt quite pleased with himself; so pleased, in fact, that he decided to take it easy.

It transpired that Dreyfus's colleagues had given him the wrong information, as he had not, after all, passed the leading car when he decided to slow right down and imagine he was taking a leisurely Sunday drive.

Crossing the line, he fully expected that winner's honours awaited him, but of course they did not. To the poor man's surprise, he was actually five minutes behind.

Rock-solid opposition

When the Swedish racing driver Bjorn Waldegaard was taking part in the 1979 Monte Carlo Rally, he found that the Villars stage had been blocked by rocks, put there by spectators.

Waldegaard's co-driver had to get out and lever the rocks away, but the Escort was denied seventy-five crucial seconds – and ultimately victory in the rally. The Lancia Stratos of Bernard Darniche of France beat the Swede by just six seconds.

And the winner is . . . and the winner is . . . and . . .

The Austrian Alpine Rally of 1974 is most notable for having three winners. Such was the confusion that, in the end, officials threw up their hands and erased the whole sorry mess from the motorsport calendar.

Achim Warmbold's BMW had the smallest number of penalty points. But the organizers disqualified him because he had approached a control from the wrong direction. However, the driver argued that the control had been in the wrong place and that the Renault team manager had blocked the route at one point, deliberately.

With Warmbold ruled out, another winner was declared. This was Bernard Darniche, driving a Renault Alpine. He was just one second ahead of Per Eklund, who was driving a Saab. The Saab team were not happy about this at all. The regulations, they said, stated that timing was to be to the whole second, but organizers had announced that the stage times would be timed to one-tenth of a second. Saab argued that, if the tenths were ignored, Eklund would have won by a second.

Long after the rally had ended and the motorsport season had moved on, these disputes were still being thrashed out until, in a blaze of bewilderment, officials decided it would be better if the race had never happened.

So it was dropped from the calendar, after expunging the results of the 1974 fixture.

The Sport of Kings

A day at the races is the ideal way to spend a summer afternoon for many. A drink in the bar, a flutter placed with one of the track bookmakers, the atmosphere, the anticipation, the excitement when a favoured horse is coming into the final furlong neck and neck with the favourite.

As with most sports, though, things can go wrong, whether through horse, jockey or trainer error. We have galloped through a number of amusing stories to bring you a colourful selection, including a couple of tales from the dog-racing world.

Dead cert

Dying in the saddle can be an awful screw-up. It happened though, in 1923, when Frank Hayes rode Sweet Kiss – a 20–1 shot – to win a steeplechase at Belmont Park at Elmont, New York.

Over the finish went horse and rider, and friends and connections went in to congratulate him, only to find him dead and slumped in the saddle.

It is the only time a dead jockey has won a race.

Off course

Marker dolls had not been placed correctly on the course during the Prince of Wales Novices' Chase at Chepstow in December 1987. The result was that the entire field took the wrong course, and crashed through a rail on to the hurdles course.

However, the racecourse executive at Chepstow paid out a share of the prize money to the owners of the twelve horses that had been wrongly diverted to a different course.

Jumped back in – and out again

Chris Warren was looking forward to getting back into his stride as a jump jockey after being out of racing for five weeks owing to a broken collarbone. His comeback was arranged for November 1988, when he would be riding Allied Force in a novices hurdle race at Newbury.

On the day, however, he discovered his car had been stolen during the night. When he eventually found the vehicle, it had been badly vandalized. Fortunately, the riding gear he had stored inside the car, ready for his big race, was still intact, so he managed to get a lift and made it to Newbury just in time.

As it turned out, Allied Force was not a force to be reckoned with on that day, and fell at the first fence. Warren suffered another fall, too, and the same collarbone was broken once again.

Unstable stable

After the poor performance that his horse, Wickham, displayed during the 1910 Grand National, Frank Bibby, Wickham's trainer, was angry and disappointed after what had been a quite promising start.

There were twenty-five runners, and almost half of them were soon out of the race, but Bibby's three horses – Wickham at 66–1 and the two stable-mates, Caubeen and Glenside – were still in contention, and this was where Wickham's unruly behaviour began. Having collided with Caubeen, sending the horse and its mount on to the turf, he ran across Glenside at a fence, bringing down himself and the other horse. Thus, thanks to Wickham, all three runners from the same stable were eliminated. The winner that year was Jenkinstown.

Bibby did score well in the following year's National, however, as Glenside won the race at 20–1.

Weighty problem

Before the race in the Netherkelly Notices' Chase, Richard Rowe had left the paddock at the correct weight, but at the weigh-in after the race he was 14 pounds (6.3 kilos) lighter. As a result of Rowe's sudden weight loss, his horse, Hogmanay, was disqualified from first place in the chase, held in November 1988.

Puzzlingly, after studying film of the race, stewards

just could not pinpoint where on the course the lead weights that had been attached to the saddle had become detached.

The question of the missing stone was never resolved.

Horseradish, anyone?

Security was perhaps not as tight in the nineteenth century as it is now. How else could a group of picnickers find themselves still sitting beneath the rail of the first fence with an entire field of racehorses thundering in their direction?

In 1871, this unlikely scenario occurred. Oblivious to the fact that a race had begun, the picnickers picnicked on and it was not until the horses were dangerously close that the group realized what was happening, and ran away from the scene without further delay.

Out to grass - voluntarily

On the day of the 1952 Goodwood Cup, Aquino II was at 2–1, and tipped to do well in the race. Unfortunately, Aquino II was a horse very much prone to lapses of concentration, and had been fitted with blinkers to ensure he was focused on the track ahead, and avoiding the distraction of the fields on either side.

Success in the race did not bode well from the start, though, as Aquino II first tried to turn around and go back to the paddock. His jockey managed to get him back on course, but the animal had only galloped for a furlong (201 metres) before swerving into the centre of the course.

Finally, when Aquino II reached a bend coming off the straight, the blinkers proved useless when the horse espied lush grass, adorned with buttercups and daisies. He waited until he saw a gap in the railings, and as soon as one came up, the horse sauntered into the field and partook of a verdant feast, oblivious to the outcome of the race.

Whacked and fagged out!

A bright hopeful called Young Whack was disqualified by the Dublin Turf Club in July 2001 after he failed a drugs test at Navan in Ireland, but the seven-year-old had never been near any stimulants.

It transpired that the drug Young Whack had been 'taking' was nicotine. His trainer, Noel Meade, could offer no clue as to how Young Whack had got a sniff of the tobacco. The stewards accepted that Meade had 'taken all reasonable precautions', but poor old Young Whack had to be disqualified nonetheless.

'He'll be some horse when we get him off the fags,' Meade quipped.

Slip Up slipped ahead

The horse that won the Devon and Exeter in 1986 – Slip Up – was fortunate not to live up to its name on this particular occasion.

Roger Charlton was riding towards the post on Amantiss and was just a few metres from the line. Suddenly, Amantiss decided to drop him on to the grass.

Amantiss was first past the post but, without its jockey, it could not be officially placed. Taking advantage of his rival's mishap, Slip Up slipped in from second place to first, and won the race.

Travel sickness

All White was a rank outsider in the 1919 Grand National. His usual rider, Robert Chadwick, was out of the race through injury, and so another jockey, T. Williams, was brought in as a substitute rider.

He needed to reduce his weight to the required level of 9 stone and 10 pounds (just under 62 kilos), and so set about fasting for several days before the ride.

However, on the day of the race, he decided to have a plate or two of cockles and mussels from a seafood stall at Aintree, but that proved to be a costly error for Mr Williams.

After a jump on the second circuit, Williams was forced to halt his mount and lean over to be violently sick. He recovered and set off again to catch up with the rest, but eventually had to settle for fifth place.

Unstable boy

It was a stable lad who made the sporting screw-up that caused the in-form horse, Manifesto, to miss out on a chance to win a consecutive Grand National in 1898.

Before this race, the horse – which had won the 1897 race, and would go on to win the National in 1899 – had been sold for £4,000 to Mr J. G. Bulteel, and he had put it in the charge of a new trainer. However, a week before the Grand National the stable lad left the door open, and Manifesto went walkabout, trying to jump a gate during his wanderings.

When he was eventually found it was discovered he had bruised his fetlock, and had to miss the race as a result.

The stable boy is said to have made himself scarce, and was never seen again after realizing his unfortunate error.

Shocking fall

When Aly Branford was found twitching after falling from his horse during a National Hunt race at Wye, ambulance staff were mystified. He had been thrown over the running rail, and his twitching could not be fathomed, until his rescuers found he had landed on an electric fence used to keep sheep from roaming.

Tell us a Knother one!

Mick Morrissey left the starting gate on a horse called Knother, but passed the post on Royal Student. The horse was not renamed halfway round the track, of course, as Morrissey actually began the race on one horse and ended it on another.

This extraordinary event happened during the two-mile steeplechase race at Southwell in 1953. At the fifth fence, Royal Student fell, not only throwing his rider off but creating an obstacle for Knother, who crashed into him, throwing Morrissey out of the saddle. Morrissey went high into the air, but landed squarely in the other horse's saddle, and it was Royal Student, and not Knother, that took him to the end of the race.

What's up, Duc?

It is hard to tell which jockey has been parted from his mount the highest number of times, but the Duke of Albuquerque must be up there with the winners – or losers, depending on how one looks at it.

He made racing history in 1963 when he was given 66–1 against finishing the Grand National while still actually in the saddle.

The Spanish aristocrat seemed to divide his time between the saddle and the stretcher, beginning the race but not usually ending it, and finding himself, instead, in the Royal Liverpool Infirmary.

He almost broke his neck in 1952, when he fell at the sixth fence, and in 1963 it was at the fourth fence that he and his horse parted company. His horse collapsed in 1965, and his stirrup broke in 1973, although he managed to cling on for eight fences before coming off.

He fell off during training in 1974, but rode with a broken collarbone and his leg in plaster.

Bang off target

Sally Oliver was looking forward to her day trip to Bangor. The Midlands trainer had a horse running there, and it came in first.

However, when the stewards required her attendance for the purpose of an enquiry, she was nowhere to be found. She was in Bangor, they were in Bangor, but it soon became apparent that they were in completely different Bangors. Bangor-on-Dee was a small village in Shropshire, where the race was being held. Bangor in North Wales, about a hundred miles away, was where Sally had journeyed, believing the race was to be held there.

Neigh, lad!

On the occasion of the New Stand Design Team Slaney Novice Hurdle at Naas in Ireland in January 1999, Paul Carberry made a mistake that cost him not only the race, but also landed him with a ten-day suspension.

He thought there was another lap to go, but he was wrong. He was riding along comfortably on Sallie's Girl, and was making no attempt to increase his pace. When he saw other horses picking up the pace at speed, he kept back tucked in behind Glazeaway, ridden by Conor O'Dwyer.

Carberry even called to O'Dwyer that there was another lap left, but O'Dwyer, wisely, chose not to take any notice. It was only when Carberry and Sallie's Girl crossed the finish line that he realized his terrible mistake.

Evening meal

Inkerman's patience was wearing thin, and he was growing tired of carrying his rider round a track. And so, in the 1863 Grand National, the horse dumped its rider and wandered off at the Canal Turn.

The horse's connections spent hours looking for the errant equine, and eventually found him, late at night, some miles away from the track at Aintree, munching grass in a field.

The napper and the nap

When Graham Bradley was struck down with tiredness on 18 May 1994, the date of a race at Worcester, he decided to have a nap in his car. He overslept, however, making him late for the race, so stewards fined him £100.

In the event, Macedonas, the horse he should have ridden, went on to win the Handley Castle Novices' Chase, ridden by Simon McNeill, the jockey who replaced Bradley.

Bradley told reporters afterwards, 'I was here an hour and a half before racing and I had a doze in the car. When I woke up, I was a minute too late to weigh out.'

The National that never was

On 3 April 1993, the 150th Aintree Martell Grand National went down in history as the race that never was, following a fiasco with the starting tape.

The race had already been disrupted when a number of demonstrators had to be removed from the first fence, but when the horses had settled, and the starter, Captain Keith Brown, called the riders into line and start the race, the strong wind caused the starting tape to become caught around one of the horses, resulting in a false start being called.

After the horses returned, settled and lined up again, another false start was called as some of the horses had been too near the tape when it lifted; Richard Dunwoody had become entwined in the tape on the back of Won't Be Gone Long. Though nine horses had pulled up before the first fence, most of the field had already set off at pace, and did not realize a false start had been signalled.

Race officials attempted to attract the attention of the riders as they reached The Chair, but were mistaken for protesters, following the earlier problems on the racecourse.

Though seven horses finished the four-and-a-half-mile race, with Esha Ness ridden by John White crossing the line first, the race was later declared void, costing the UK Treasury and betting industry millions of pounds.

Blood, Mud and Machismo

Ever since William Webb Ellis invented the game of rugby, the sport has thrilled spectators all over the world. And none more so than in the nations associated with it: England, Wales, Ireland, France, Scotland, Australia, New Zealand, South Africa . . .

A game of hulking men, lots of spills, rough and tough scrums, kicking, running, and passing an oval ball about the field, with its fair share of blood, mud and machismo.

It has its lighter moments, of course, as the next few entries wholeheartedly prove.

Unrepeatable event

Not a tale to make a Welshman feel proud, but the consolation is that this incident did happen a long time ago.

Back in 1881 at Blackheath, England and Wales turned up for a rugby union international, but Wales had arrived in London two players short; the men's invitations had gone astray. So two university players were quickly recruited, but failed to muster the quality of the missing players, even though they both had Welsh qualifications.

It appears that the Welsh side was so humiliated by the circumstances that the fixture at Blackheath was never repeated.

Laughing Boy

Rugby is usually taken so seriously by its fans and players, so on the occasion of South Africa's visit to New Zealand, to take on the All Blacks in 1937, the sight of a grown man giggling like a naughty schoolboy was a rare thing to behold.

The Springboks' player Boy Louw had suffered a blow to the head that had resulted in a bout of concussion, and so he barely knew where he was for the rest of the match. Disorientation apart, he found himself unable to stop giggling; most unheard of on a rugby pitch.

During one of his fits of laughter, Louw broke off from the game and asked his captain, Danie Craven, what was happening and what he ought to be doing. Craven suggested he should try to stop the All Blacks' prop, Dalton, from coming through the lineout.

So, at the next lineout, Boy charged into Dalton while the referee was looking the other way, giggling as he did so and looking to his captain for approval.

The Springboks did manage to win the match 13–6, however, in spite of laughing Boy's unpredictable, yet amusing, behaviour.

Nice try!

While playing for Kukris against Panaga, Dick Dover scooped up a loose ball as he broke away from the scrum, dashed 75 yards with it and touched down for a try. Thinking it strange that no one had challenged him en route, he realized he had placed the ball under the posts of his own team, having become disorientated while in the scrum and run the wrong way . . .

Own goal (posts)

When one's rugby union club is told to leave its ground to make way for a league club, the response will never be well-received.

It happened to Bridgend RFC in South Wales when they were told they would have to leave their Brewery Field home in 1948.

They had the last laugh, however, after creeping on to the field under cover of darkness and stealing the goalposts.

Stick-in-the-mud rescue

Rugby pitches can become veritable quagmires sometimes. None less so than during the match between Taranaki of New Zealand and the British Lions in 1977.

When Dave Loveridge of Taranaki sustained a bad knee injury, the stretcher, the usual means of taking a player off for first aid, was deemed inappropriate, and an ambulance was called for.

As a result of the horrendous conditions underfoot, the

vehicle got well and truly stuck in the mud, and it was eighteen minutes before both players and spectators could free the wheels and get the vehicle on its way with the injured player snug inside.

No ball!

In 1966, the Colwyn Bay rugby team went to North Wales to play their rivals Porthmadog. The field was set, the crowd waited in breathless anticipation, the teams lined up opposite each other, the touch judges were in place, the referee was ready for the kick-off, the ball was . . .

Despite all efforts to find a ball, not one could be found, and so the match had to be abandoned.

Sock it to 'em, John

When John Roberts turned up to play for Cardiff Athletic against Chepstow in 1937, he had a vital piece of kit missing – his boots.

However, Roberts had set his heart on playing and retaining his place in the Cardiff first team. So he played in just his socks.

Such lip!

Peter Harvey was a scrum-half for Canterbury, New Zealand, and had been chosen to play in an All Blacks tour of Britain in 1905.

He was unable to fulfil his obligation to the famous national side, however, because the prime minister of New Zealand refused to allow him to leave the country. The reason was that he was the only qualified lip reader in the islands.

Light entertainment

Strange though it sounds, some sports fixtures were actually floodlit in the nineteenth century.

In a match between the Scottish Borders towns of Hawick and Melrose on a snowy night in 1879, some 5,000 spectators gathered to watch one of the earliest lit games. Not surprisingly, lighting was not as sophisticated then as it is now, and lighting outside the ground was clearly inadequate to stop a number of people sneaking in without paying.

As soon as the match ended, perhaps to save electricity or to punish the gatecrashers, officials turned out the lights, leaving fans to fumble about and crawl over one another to get out of the stadium; not only in darkness, but in snowy slush, too.

Not settling the score

At Twickenham in 1933, England were playing Wales – always a clash that generates patriotic pride. A kick at the goal by Vivian Jenkins went 'at least a yard outside the right-hand post', according to the *Daily Telegraph*. But the Welsh touch-judge raised his flag to show he thought the ball had passed between the posts. The English touch-judge did not agree, however.

The result was that the scoreboard carried the wrong score for the rest of the match. Spectators thought Wales had won 9–3 when they had in fact won only 7–3.

Ripping yarn

During scrums and the general rough and tumble of a competitive rugby match, players' shorts are occasionally very badly ripped. When this happens, the usual procedure is for a ring of players to form a circle around the player with the ruined shorts so he can change into a fresh pair.

Not so for the Australian captain Trevor Allen when his side were playing at Twickenham against England during the 1947–8 tour. He threw convention to the wind, whipped off the damaged garment and walked to an attendant several metres away to get a new pair of shorts, jockstrap on full view, in front of a crowd that included a royal party.

As one would expect, there were those who like to create a fuss over such things, and there were mutterings within the world of rugby union for some time.

Streak of bad luck

In the 1970s there was a TV documentary that recorded the achievements of a rugby team from Doncaster in South Yorkshire. During its history, the side came bottom of its league more times than any other club, and lost forty games on the trot.

On one occasion the players failed to recognize their own strip because they were covered in mud, and began to tackle their own side.

The entire team was put up for sale in 1980.

Word play

Fly-halfs usually pay very close attention to the game and play an important role in the proceedings, but when Mick English was playing for Ireland against England in 1958, his opposite number Phil Horrocks-Taylor

managed to run past him and score a try to clinch the
match for the English.

His teammates asked him what had happened, and he
replied, 'Well the Horrocks went one way and the Taylor
went the other, and I was left holding the hyphen.'

Late arrivals

Mombasa Rugby Football Club boarded a plane in 1974
and flew 475 miles to Uganda for their annual needle
match with Nairobi Harlequins. What they were unaware
of was that several thousand feet below them, travelling
in the opposite direction, were a fleet of cars bound for
Mombasa.

Each team, once it had arrived, rang the other to find
out where it had got to, to discover the unfortunate mix-
up.

Putting the boot in (his shorts)

Sid Going was an All Blacks half-back who, playing for
North Auckland, claimed some of the credit for his
side's 35-point win over Buller, to win New Zealand's
Ranfurly Shield.

The going for Going was good in the 1972 match, and
the Buller lads were clearly affected by this man's
amazing skill. During a tackle, however, Going lost a
boot, and a Buller lock, Orlando Nahr, slipped it into his
shorts while no one was looking.

Since no one knew where the missing boot was, Going
had to play the rest of the game wearing only one boot.

The luck of the Irish!

Ireland had embarked on a centenary tour of New Zealand in 1975, and had arranged to drop by to play a game against Fiji en route.

Unfortunately, the Fijians were not at home when the Irish team landed – they had left the country to begin a tour of Australia.

The (bad) luck of the draw

While making the draw for the 1995 World Cup, the procedure had to be carried out three times.

The first draw, made in January 1993, did not please Australia and New Zealand, because they said teams from the same pool should not meet again until the final.

The officials agreed, and a second draw was made. But then there was a printing error, which meant that teams from the same pool would still meet before the final.

Eventually, at the third attempt, the draw was made successfully to the satisfaction of all concerned.

Troubled waters

Scotland's W. A. Allan was appointed to referee the
Ireland–New Zealand international in Dublin in 1935,
but had not reckoned on the Irish Sea slowing him
down.

He set off in good time or so he thought, but
encountered some rather lively weather, and was still
stranded at sea when the match kicked off. So a
substitute referee was sent on – R. W. Jeffares, son of
the secretary of the Irish Rugby Football Union.

!#**#@}%, ref!

Newton Abbott player Denys Dobson was a pleasant
fellow, really, but he had an unfortunate habit of being
sent off, which was a shame, because he had already
earned six caps as an England forward.

The reason for his numerous dismissals was owing to
his consistent use of obscene language directed at the
referee.

Dobson received an eight-month suspension for one
such display during a British Lions tour of Australia and
New Zealand in 1904.

Compared with the treatment meted out to a referee
in Peru, however, Dobson's behaviour was positively
saintly. Felipe Compinez awarded a penalty during a
local cup competition but, when the goal was scored,
angry fans of the other team stormed the pitch and
stoned Compinez to death.

Printer's devil

A slip-up of an editorial kind appeared in the matchday
programme for an Ireland–France international in 1980,
when the surname of the Irish back Colm Tucker was
found to begin with an 'F' instead of a 'T'.

Slipped disc

It was the day of the draw for the first round of the
1923–4 Rugby League Challenge Cup competition.
Teams were drawn using cardboard discs.

All went well until the draw was almost over. When the
officials drawing the balls got to Salford, it seemed that
they would be at home to no one, for there was no disc
left in the bag for the away team. Strangely, thirty-two
discs had been placed in the bag and yet only thirty-one
had been drawn out.

Not only was the Salford team mystified, but so was
Hunslet, because their name had yet to be drawn.

Eventually, it emerged that the disc with Hunslet's
name on it had slipped out earlier in the draw, having
become stuck to the back of Swinton's disc, and gone
unnoticed by officials.

The League decided to give Hunslet the away tie with
Salford, since it was the only possible pairing left.
Hunslet did not agree with the idea, but were denied a
re-draw.

Aye, aye – anyone eyed my eye?

The 14-stone (89-kilogram) forward Steve Bush,
playing for Silverhill Colliery, Nottinghamshire,
managed to lose his glass eye during a game of rugby.

Silverhill were playing Daw Mill Colliery of
Warwickshire in the 1993 Coal Board Cup, and the
game had to be held up for a while after Bush had been
spotted looking for something after a hard scrum.

When the referee, Peter Llewellyn, asked him what he
had lost, Bush replied, 'My eye.' At first Llewellyn
thought that a hospital visit was required, but Bush
reassured him it was just his glass eye.

In spite of much searching through the grass, the glass
eye, which had probably been stamped into the ground

during the scrum, could not be found, and so Bush had to play with an empty socket for the rest of the match.

Whether or not it was down to the fact that Bush was turning a blind eye, Silverhill lost 17–8.

Early bath - then play again

Referees have been known to blow the whistle at the wrong time, but are usually only ever out by a few seconds or the odd minute. When East Midlands were playing Barbarians at Northampton in 1921, however, the referee's watch proved to be far less than accurate.

Adrian Stoop, a former England international player, blew the whistle for the end of the play fourteen minutes early.

Whatever the reason for the players' early bath, they were ordered out on to the field again to complete the game.

Adding insult to injury

An incident during the third round of the Rugby League Challenge Cup tie between Swinton and Castleford during the 1927–8 season led to a change in the rules.

One of the Swinton players had been hurt and was being treated off the pitch, so Castleford thought they could take advantage of having one extra man. At one point, Castleford's side, en masse, swamped the Swinton line and it looked as if they were about to score a try.

They were thwarted, however, when a player emerged from nowhere and executed a perfect tackle, preventing the try. Castleford players, robbed of this golden opportunity, could only look around in bewilderment at where the mysterious tackler had come from.

It was the injured player. He had seen the danger, decided he had to act quickly, fought the pain, ran on to the pitch and made the tackle. The Castleford team was outraged, and protested loudly, but judgment was against them. They even went on to lose the match.

Eventually, the rules were changed to state that injured players need to be given permission to return to the field.

Getting carried away

Rugby is a game that produces many injuries, but France's Jean-Pierre Salut must have set something of a record, for he was carried off before he even got on the pitch.

He was about to take part in an 1969 international against Scotland in Paris, and was running up the stairs from the dressing room ready to make his entry on to the pitch. But he fell and broke his ankle, and was stretchered away.

And now a word from our sponsor . . .

It could happen only in America. John Reardon was refereeing a match between England and Mid-West at Cleveland, Ohio, in June 1982, when suddenly the match stopped dead, on Reardon's orders.

The English players wondered what on earth was happening, when Reardon told them he had been instructed to stop play because a local TV station was covering the fixture, and at this point they had to show advertisements.

Torn between making money from advertising revenue and ensuring that TV viewers did not miss vital play, the TV company had done a deal to have the game stopped whenever the ads were due to be broadcast.

Cap that!

Arnold Alcock, who played for Guy's Hospital, could be excused for wondering why he was so special when he was sent an invitation to play for England at rugby. The great event that would earn him his first and only cap was a match against South Africa in 1906.

The reason Alcock received his call-up paper, however, was due to a clerical error. The invitation should have gone to Lancelot Slocock, who played for Liverpool.

Alcock's big game proved to be his only international outing, as he was completely out of his depth. Slocock, on the other hand, played for his country eight times.

Celebratory trickle

Great Britain won the inaugural Rugby League World Cup, held in France in 1954. And, of course, a celebration was called for.

Naturally, the trophy, which was presented by the French Rugby League, was filled with champagne, but it soon became apparent that there was a leak. The cup had not been made watertight where the handles joined the bowl.

Drunk and incapable

Corby rugby team were on a tour of northern England in 1989.

After a heavy night on the town the previous day, they staggered manfully on to the field of play to take on Whitby. The referee soon realized that most of the Corby side were too drunk to play and so he abandoned the match.

To clear up any doubt on the matter of their sobriety, the scoreline of 80–0 provided ample proof.

Couldn't bank on it

It was a proud day for Frank Clayton in 1884. He had
been selected for the first New Zealand tour to
Australia.

At the bank where he worked, his bosses would not
believe him when he told them of his selection and they
refused to give him the time off.

Sorry, mate, you'll have to pay

As the referee of an important match, it is most unusual
to be charged an admission fee to enter the ground, but
Cyril Gadney found himself in this awkward situation
on the day of the 1936 international between Wales and
Ireland at Cardiff.

As time went by, and the match was nearing kick-off,
officials began to worry why the English referee was
nowhere to be seen. They waited a while longer and
were wondering what contingency plans they might
make, when Gadney was seen queuing up to get in, and
having to pay for the privilege.

He had arrived at the ground in good time and told
the gateman he was the referee, but the gateman refused
to believe him, thinking it was a likely story, made up to
gain free entry to the ground.

So it was that Gadney had to queue with the
spectators, much to the embarrassment of Cardiff's
stadium officials.

I'm off, by George!

It was all too overwhelming for George Crawford, as he refereed Bristol's match against Newport in September 1985.

The clash soon deteriorated into a mass brawl, and Crawford could neither control it nor put up with it. So he walked off, and a local official had to take his place for the rest of the game.

In need of air

The United States of America were playing their first rugby union international match since defeating France in the final of the 1924 Olympic Games in Paris.

But the Americans, taking on Australia in Los Angeles, had made some fundamental errors. The pitch was neither long enough, nor wide enough. Furthermore, it was not marked properly. The ball felt like a soggy balloon and was badly in need of inflation. Eventually, after an announcement over the PA, a pump was produced, the ball was properly inflated and the match got under way.

Despite the earlier problems, the Australians remained focused, and achieved a 24–12 victory.

Time out

Referee John Cail was rather embarrassed when he officiated in New Zealand's match against Yorkshire during the Maoris' tour of Britain in 1888–9, because his watch had ceased to function, and so he had to go into the crowd and borrow one that worked.

Putting the Boot In

Football is fast, furious, fantastic, and extremely tribal.
Some would say it is the best spectator sport as
adrenalin pumps through the body while chants are
chanted, anthems sung, scarves waved. Nothing excites
the sporting public quite like football, and we seem to
cry out for more and more of it as television viewers.

Football is also a serious money-making business, with
record transfer fees and players' salaries growing ever
higher. It's not all serious, though, as there are many
hilarious stories concerning players, referees and
spectators alike whose embarrassing stories have taken
up thousands of column inches in local and national
newspapers.

Mismatch

In 1973, a Wolverhampton Sunday League team, Oxbarn Social Club, arranged a friendly match in Germany, reasoning that it would be a good chance to have a holiday and hone their playing skills at the same time.

They were expecting to play on a recreation ground, so it was not until they arrived at their opponents' luxury stadium that they realized they had arranged a match with a top German side. SVW Mainz, a first-division team, were expecting to play Wolverhampton Wanderers, who were at the time one of Britain's top teams.

The Oxbarn club's secretary told journalists at the time, 'I thought it looked posh, and when I heard the other side were on an eight-pound bonus to win, I said to myself, "Something's wrong."'

The Oxbarn goalkeeper was seen to fall to his knees, as if praying for the match to end, after the fifteenth ball had sailed past him and into the net. The final score was SVW Mainz 21 Oxbarn Social Club 0, but the British side was glad of the practice.

Rio felt not too grand

Injuries can happen when they are least expected – not always on the field.

In the case of the world's most expensive defender, England international Rio Ferdinand, he managed to strain a tendon in his knee in January 2001. He was not playing for his club, Leeds United, at the time, but was sitting in front of the television with his feet up.

His then manager, David O'Leary, explained to reporters: 'It was a freak accident, and typical of this season. It wasn't even on the training ground. He was watching television and had his foot up on the coffee table. He had it there in a certain position for a number of hours . . . and strained a tendon behind his knee.'

Unlucky for some

The number thirteen has long been regarded as an unlucky number by the superstitious. It proved to be so in another way for the match between Leicester City and Stockport County in May 1921, which managed a crowd of just thirteen.

The explanation for the lack of support was that both teams were playing away from home, because Stockport's ground had been temporarily closed. The match was held, instead, at Old Trafford, the home of Manchester United.

Netted

Chick Brodie was goalkeeper for Brentford in the late 1960s, and on one occasion was playing in an away game at Lincoln City in the Fourth Division.

He was responding to a high cross and thought it would be a good idea to stop the ball from going into the top of the goal by hanging on to the crossbar. However, with an ear-splitting crack, the crossbar snapped and down came Brodie, ensuring that he and two defenders got tangled up in the netting.

The match had to be suspended for forty-five minutes while repairs were carried out. Perhaps not helped by Brodie's unconventional goalkeeping, Brentford went on to lose 2–0.

Window of opportunity

According to the *Sun* newspaper in February 2002, it is vital for Norwich City that a window cleaner's sponge is present at the ground on match days, because without it they cannot win.

The Canaries had won on twelve occasions in the 2001–2002 season when window cleaner, Keith Adams, had cleaned windows there, but when he was somewhere else, the team could only draw four matches and lose one.

It is fortunate that Adams's boss is a Norwich fan, for he ensures that the window cleaner is always at the ground on match days.

Franc exchange

At the beginning of a 1950 club match in France, one of the captains accidentally swallowed the five-franc piece that was being used to decide which team played at which end first.

Rules were made to be exploited

In a match played between Barbados and Grenada in a cup match in February 1994, the Barbadian players faced being knocked out of the competition unless they won the game by two clear goals. However, there was also a draft rule in the competition, which stated that in the event of a draw the game would go to penalty kicks, and the winner of the penalty shoot-out would be awarded a 2–0 victory.

With five minutes left on the clock Barbados were leading 2–1, but without the vital two-goal lead over their opposition, the team was on the verge of an early exit from the tournament.

Accepting that it would be a difficult task to score

against Grenada's mass of defenders, they turned round, advanced on their own defence, and deliberately scored an own goal to produce a 2–2 draw, intending to take the game into penalties. The Grenadian players immediately realized the opposing team's tactics, and swiftly responded by attempting to score an own goal themselves.

The Barbados team was quick to start defending the opposition's goal, however, to prevent Grenada's one-goal lead from being restored. With just minutes to go, spectators witnessed the farcical sight of both team's defending their opponent's goal against attackers desperately trying to score an own goal and goalkeepers trying to throw the ball into their own net.

The Grenadian players were unable to produce a goal before the final whistle blew, and so the 2–2 draw meant the game went to penalties. Barbados was victorious and so recorded a 2–0 victory against the unfortunate Grenadian side, and progressed to the next round.

You're out of line

When a team named Over Wallop Reserves played a side representing a local pub called the Lardicake, the match was far from dull when a replacement referee was needed for the match in the Andover and District Sunday League. As a qualified referee, Over Wallop's manager, Terry Gilligan, agreed to officiate.

During the game, the linesman, Phil Cooper, was rather aggrieved when Gilligan ignored his flag for a foul and signalled for the match to continue. When Gilligan did eventually stop play, it was to order Cooper off the pitch for behaviour most unsuitable for a linesman. Cooper refused to go, so Gilligan abandoned the match with his own side leading 1–0. Cooper was eventually fined by the Hampshire FA and suffered a ninety-one-day suspension.

Damaged goods

It is always a joy to receive a cup after winning a coveted title or a competition, but sometimes joy can turn to overexcitement. In the case of Charlton manager, Jimmy Seed, whose team won the 1947 FA Cup Final, he accidentally dropped the gleaming trophy, damaging the lid.

The cup was due to be paraded at a civic reception, so emergency repairs had to be carried out quickly at a local garage.

Twenty-four years later, it was Liverpool's reserve team coach, Phil Thompson, who damaged the lid of the FA Cup. He left his team's London hotel after the final, and managed to drop the lid, damaging it so badly that it would not fit back on the cup itself.

Pick a card, any card

It is rare for a football match to turn into a card game, but in a match between River and Oeiras in the State League of Piaui, north-east Brazil, in early 2002, Paulo Araujo was 'carded' five times by the referee Edmilson Timoteo da Silva.

Araujo's 'hand' consisted of two yellows (for two separate fouls), followed by a red, which sent him off the pitch. Another yellow followed because he had remained on the pitch, unbeknown to the referee, who had not spotted him until he needed to give him a second yellow card for a foul. The final red card followed automatically.

The official reason why the referee had not realized that Paulo was still on the field was because he thought that many players looked alike.

'I consider this a serious mistake,' announced Edson Rezende, president of refereeing within CBF, the Brazilian Football Confederation.

The referee said, 'I've never seen anything like it. People even said I'm going to get a place at the Guinness Book [of Records] for the amount of cards I gave.'

Seeing red

Melvin Sylvester was a football referee, and a good one by all accounts. He knew the rules, and as far as he was concerned, the only penalty for someone caught punching a player was an immediate sending-off.

In April 1998, forty-two-year-old Sylvester was overseeing an Andover and District Sunday League match between the Southampton Arms and Hurstbourne Tarrant British Legion. He had stepped in when the official referee was taken ill. In a moment of sheer madness, however, he lost his temper and threw a punch at one of the players, and had no choice but to send himself off.

Sylvester had reacted a little too hastily to what he thought was a push by a Hurstbourne player, saying he was 'sorely provoked'. 'I punched him after he had pushed me from behind,' said Sylvester. 'He then swore. I just couldn't take any more. I blew my top.'

So he gave himself a red card and a spectator substituted for him for the rest of the match.

Not the final whistle, then

There were just seconds left until the end of the match when Arsenal played Blackpool at Highbury in 1955. Arsenal were winning 4–0 and their left-back, Dennis

Evans, heard a whistle. Thinking it was the referee, Frank
Coultas, blowing for the end of the game, Evans casually
flicked the ball into his own net. His goalkeeper had also
assumed that he had heard the final whistle, and began
picking up his cap and gloves.

In actual fact, the whistle had been blown by a spectator,
so the referee had to award Blackpool a goal.

On me 'ead, Bill

In 1898, during a game between Sheffield United and
Liverpool at Anfield, United player Bill 'Fatty' Foulke
responded aggressively to the shoulder charge inflicted on
him by Liverpool player, George Allan.

Known for his explosive temper, Foulke picked Allan up
by the ankles and stood him on his head in the mud,
before bouncing him up and down to make his point.

A thirsty game

During a ninety-minute game, footballers naturally get
thirsty. In August 1979, the players in a match between
Winthorpe Wanderers and British Seedhouses, held at
Newark in Nottinghamshire, decided they wanted a drink.
There was a handy container at the side of the pitch, and
so they took their fill.

The players should have checked the contents more
closely, however, for the container also held Paraquat (a
weedkiller) and a corrosive acid the groundsman used for
burning holes in the pitch.

Eleven players needed hospital treatment but,
fortunately, none of them were seriously hurt. They were
mercilessly teased for weeks afterwards, though.

Leg before goal

To score one own goal is unfortunate; to score two own goals seems like carelessness. For Herbie Roberts of Arsenal, the unthinkable happened during a match at Highbury against Derby County in October 1932.

While attacking from the Clock End during the early part of the game, Derby's left-winger, Dally Duncan, sent a hanging ball across the field, and Herbie stuck out his leg. Unfortunately, the ball hit it and went into the net.

After the restart, spectators saw what television viewers decades later would call an instant replay. Duncan centred a ball, and Herbie was there again. In went the ball for a second own goal.

It may have been small compensation for Herbie that the match ended not with disaster for his side, but a more respectable 3–3 draw.

The power of prayer

There have been many odd reasons for failure, but the excuse offered by Senhor Isadore Irandir of the Brazilian side Rio Preto stands alone. He let in a goal after just three seconds of play when his side were up against Corinthians at Bahia Stadium. From the kick-off, the ball went to Roberto Riveline, who drove it with a powerful left foot from the halfway line. It went straight past Irandir's head.

His excuse was that he was still on his knees in the goalmouth doing his pre-match prayers.

Own goal (1)

During a match against Liverpool in 1960, Charlton winger Sam Lawrie, in a moment of distraction, decided to pass the ball back to his goalkeeper.

The goalkeeper, Reed, was looking the other way at the time, however, and Lawrie had to stand horrified as the ball made its slow and infuriating way into the back of the net.

Own goals (2 and 3)

In just four days, Tommy Wright, an Everton defender, managed to score two own goals, and each came in the first minute of its respective match. He scored one in a Merseyside derby against Liverpool on 4 March, and managed to repeat the feat in an away game against Manchester United.

Absent friends

Brighton's goalkeeper, Perry Digweed, did not appear for his team's match against Bournemouth in the Second Division in September 1988 because no one had told him he was playing.

In similar circumstances the West Bromwich Albion striker Fabian de Freitas was not around when his side played Crewe on Easter Monday 1999, as he thought it was an evening kick-off.

Teammates and officials tried to contact him by phone, but the line was engaged during a lengthy call held by his girlfriend. West Brom went on to lose the match.

The Gillingham captain Mark Weatherley was prepared to be loyal to his side at all costs when snow drifts looked like preventing him from getting to the game. He trudged six miles to get to the FA Cup tie against Wigan in 1986, and when he arrived at the ground it was only to discover that the match had been called off.

The name's Bond – but don't tell anyone!

Shrewsbury Town's manager John Bond understandably feared for his safety in 1992 when his team played at Burnley. Before his current post, he had had a spell in charge at Turf Moor, and had received threats from Burnley fans, who were not at all impressed with his performance for their beloved club.

So when Shrewsbury played his former club, officials thought he would be safer if he disguised himself as a steward, watching the game from the back of the stand.

Despite the elaborate disguise, Bond's team lost 2–1.

Sprake's progress

Gary Sprake was a talented, if erratic, Welsh international goalkeeper who played for Leeds United. During a 1967 title match against Liverpool at Anfield the ball rolled to Sprake. He was about to throw it wide to Terry Cooper, but Cooper shouted to him, 'No, no!' because he could see an opposing player bearing down on him.

'So,' Sprake said, when looking back on the match many years later, 'I went to pull the ball back to my chest, as I often did, and it just flew over my left shoulder into the net.'

His teammates were blissfully unaware of their goalkeeper's slip-up, but suddenly heard a cry from the crowd. Sprake was standing on the edge of the 18-yard box with his face in his hands.

The disc jockey selecting the music for half-time played the Des O'Connor ballad, 'Careless Hands'.

Unlucky Star

In the training ground of Red Star Belgrade, fans were so angered by their team's poor performance in their country's premier league that they launched a physical attack on the team.

Red Star, who were defending champions in early 2002, trailed nine points behind their traditional rival, the first-ranking Partizan Belgrade. The fans did not like it at all, so they shouted obscenities and told players they brought shame on the club. Masked assailants then chased players into the locker room and set about them with sticks, causing police to intervene.

One of the club's midfielders, Mihajlo Pjanovic, told journalists, 'Red Star has been in crises, but this is no way to solve problems.'

The fans' behaviour was not dissimilar to that of Lazio's supporters in Rome. Not long before the Belgrade incident, they too confronted players because of their poor performance in the Italian Serie A.

What a mouth!

Alex Stepney, in goal for Manchester United during a match away to Birmingham City in 1975, had a reputation for his vocal strengths on the pitch.

He shouted so enthusiastically and energetically to his teammates that he had to be taken to hospital with a dislocated jaw.

Hand in glove with the law

How do you turn a sporting screw-up into a superstition? By leaving your goalkeeper's gloves behind.

When Jack Fairbrother (Newcastle United's goalkeeper when they won the FA Cup in 1951) managed to lose his gloves, he borrowed a pair from an obliging policeman who was patrolling the ground and passing behind the goal.

Newcastle won the match, and Fairbrother decided that, from then on, he would wear policemen's white gloves, and was said to be a frequent visitor to the police station in Market Street.

Colour blind

In the 1930–1 season, a Sheffield team was playing in an annual game against a Glasgow side.

Sheffield's captain, Jimmy Seed, kept passing the ball to the referee, but for a good reason. The referee was wearing a white shirt, and so were Seed's teammates.

Consequently the referee was persuaded to go to the dressing room and put a stop to the confusion by changing into a dark shirt.

Doppelclanger

Mick Pullen of Bognor Regis Town could be excused for not knowing what was happening when he was sent off for no reason in the 1992–3 season in the Diadora League.

After Mick's twin brother Paul had been involved in a scuffle with opponents, the referee sent Mick off instead. Despite protests of Mick's innocence the referee refused to back down.

As the team's player-manager, Mick was in a good

position to dictate matters after the incident. He said, 'Paul thought it was hilarious, but I'll make sure he serves the three-match suspension!'

Point taken

The Wheatsheaf pub team from St Helen's, Bishop Auckland, in Durham earned one point by drawing just one match out of the thirty they played during the 1994–5 season. They lost the other twenty-nine games.

Unfortunately they were docked two points because on one occasion they failed to field a team, which meant that they finished the season at the bottom of the league with an improbable 'minus one point'.

The team secretary, Gordon Heseltine, who also played centre-half, told reporters, 'This has to be the worst season in history. I can't remember anyone ever ending up in the red before. It's pretty embarrassing, but at least we know we can't get any worse!'

Bottled-up anger

Fans were far from pleased in March 1969 when Palermo lost a match 3–2 against Napoli.

They decided to vent their anger on the referee and his linesmen by throwing bottles. The referee and the other officials had to be rescued by a police helicopter, before the 5,000 furious fans could cause them any serious damage.

Flag of convenience

Phil Boyce was about to referee a local soccer match in Shrewsbury, when he managed to lock himself in the changing rooms, and become stranded there, wondering what on earth he should do.

It was fortunate for Boyce that he had a linesman's flag to hand. He waved it furiously out of the window until someone saw it, and he was freed from his predicament. The match eventually got under way after a twenty-minute delay.

Two Kevins and an Alf

In 1973, during a World Cup qualifier between England and Poland at Wembley, England desperately needed a goal. Sir Alf Ramsey decided he wanted to send Kevin Hector on to the field as a substitute, and said, 'Kevin, get stripped.'

It was Kevin Keegan, though, who heard the great man's command, and began to remove his tracksuit.

When Ramsey realized his instructions had been misheard, he tried to repeat his original request, but it was too late. By the time Hector did get on to the pitch, there were only ninety seconds of the game to play, so neither Kevin managed to have any effect.

Celebration today, injuries to Morrow

Celebrations can sometimes be more dangerous than the match itself. In the 1993 Littlewood's Cup Final between Sheffield Wednesday and Arsenal, Steve Morrow, the Northern Ireland international, scored the winning goal.

With a sense of elation, a jubilant Tony Adams hoisted Morrow into the air, but then dropped him. Morrow suffered a broken shoulder.

A spell of mayhem

An allegation of witchcraft arose when a Nairobi goalkeeper threw a cap into his goal. It was 1973, during a match between Abaluhya and Hakati. The Abaluhya side thought that the cap that the Hakati goalkeeper had thrown to the back of the net represented a spell, and would make the Hakati goal impenetrable. They alleged that an old coin, some crushed herbs, a needle, some animal skin, some roots and leaves were sewn into the band of the cap – an effective combination.

About halfway through the match, one of the Abaluhya players ran into the Hakati goal and snatched the cap, running with it to the touchline. He was chased by the entire Hakati team. The result was chaos, and the match was abandoned.

Witch way to sporting success

In April 2002, the repayment of a ten-year-old debt was finally promised to witch doctors who were thought to have put a hex on the Ivory Coast football team.

The witch doctors, from a village called Akradio, were called to help the team to victory at the 1992 African Nations Cup, but claimed not to have been properly rewarded for their skills. It was then believed that they had put a jinx on the team as punishment, as over a ten-year period the Ivory Coast achieved nothing in the African Nations Cup.

After the Ivory Coast team had performed badly in the 2000 African Nations Cup, they were sent to a military camp as a punishment and forced to frogmarch and go to lectures on patriotism. In the 2002 finals in Mali, the team were knocked out again in the first round.

As a last resort, in an effort to placate the Akradio witch doctors, the Ivory Coast's defence and civil protection minister, Moise Lida Kouassi, promised the village a bottle of spirits and the equivalent of £1,400 during a visit to the village in April 2002.

Meanwhile, in Chile, a bottom-of-the-table team, Deportes Arica, employed a witch in early 2002 to help them to escape relegation to the second division. They hired Eliana Merino to cast out 'evil spirits' from the dressing room, the stadium and the players' kit.

The ritual involved candles and smoke to 'purify' the team before kick-off. One of the team's defenders, Marcelo Muñoz, said, 'When you're at the bottom of the table, you'll do anything to improve your position.'

In 2002 the bishop of Oxford agreed to exorcise a football stadium to try to lift a 'gypsy's curse'. Oxford United's chaplain called in the Right Reverend Richard Harries after the team's poor run of results.

A moose, a-loose

Football players often collide with one another on the field, both in matches and in training.

The former Norwegian international defender, Svein Grondalen, was involved in a collision with a difference when out on an early-morning jog with a friend, when he injured himself colliding with a moose.

Becks backs a loser

At his 26th-birthday photocall in 2001, David Beckham made a huge mistake when he wore a hooded top with a picture of a face on it. Unbeknown to him, he was sporting a picture of Adolf Eichmann, the Nazi official responsible for the murder of millions of Jews.

Becks vowed he would never wear the top – sent to him by a US fan – again after the photocall at his in-laws' home in Hertfordshire.

Blowin' in the wind

It was a windy day when Newcastle United had begun checking into their hotel ready for their match at Brighton in November 1989. They were taking kit from the team coach when a gust of wind got behind the trolley containing the pile of kit baskets, and sent it hurtling down the prom. Coming the other way was a Number 67 bus, and shorts, shirts and jockstraps went flying.

United beat Brighton 3–0, further alienating the local populace.

Can we have our ball back, please?

Wolverhampton Wanderers' Peter Knowles was in a celebratory mood after a goal against Portsmouth at Fratton Park. In his excitement he gave the ball a hefty kick and sent it out of the ground.

It was never found, and because Portsmouth were so short of money at the time, they sent him a bill for a new one.

Stamp of disapproval (1)

Even the world of philately is not immune from slip-ups of a sporting kind. In Norway, the postal service printed 1.3 million stamps bearing a picture of the wrong man.

The stamp commemorated the National Soccer Federation's centenary and was supposed to show Lars Johan Hammer, a twenty-seven-year-old referee, but the man on the stamp bore no resemblance to Hammer whatsoever.

It was not until the end of March 2002, that the man on the stamp was identified as a German referee, Peter Hertel, from SG Borussia Fuerstenwalde in

Brandenburg, who presided over the Junior Norwegian Cup in 1997 alongside Hammer.

Hammer was philosophical about it. 'I don't have glasses or a beard,' he said, 'and I must say I was stunned to see this strange referee on the stamps.'

A spokeswoman for the postal service, Elisabeth Gjoelme, said the incident was embarrassing. 'When we bought the photo it was in good faith that it was the right one,' she said.

Before Hertel was identified, the postal service launched a campaign, including a veritable wanted poster in the Oslo-based Verdens Gang, Norway's largest newspaper, to discover the identity of the impostor.

The stamp was issued, complete with the wrong image, in April 2002.

Stamp of disapproval (2)

In 2002, stamps issued in the small European republic of San Marino were printed with the wrong scores to celebrate Italian footballing victories.

According to the stamps, Italy beat Czechoslovakia 4–2 to win the 1934 World Cup in Rome, but the correct score was 2–1.

Furthermore the stamps stated that Italy beat Hungary 1–0 in the 1938 World Cup Final in Paris, when they actually won 4–2.

There were six stamps in the set issued in the run-up to the World Cup and, when the error was discovered in early 2002, the postal service said they were working to release a new set, featuring the correct scores.

Deciding shot

It was a single goal that settled a 1968 match in the Third Division between Plymouth Argyle and Barrow, but it was scored by the referee.

There were just ten minutes to go, and Barrow were awarded a corner kick. The ball was kicked by a Plymouth defender, but intercepted by Barrow's George McLean, who took a shot, but it was wide; so wide, in fact, that it sailed towards the referee who was standing 11 metres from the goalmouth.

In all fairness, the referee saw the ball coming and tried to get out of the way, but it bounced off his foot and went into the goal.

The referee had no choice but to award the goal to Barrow.

Don't publish – and be damned

Back in 1936, the Football League was not a supporter of the pools companies, believing that they introduced a disreputable element into the game. In an effort to try and hamper the pools companies' business, they refused to publish fixtures. Posters for forthcoming matches would therefore advertise 'Manchester United versus ?'

Not only did this policy confuse the fans, but also the clubs. Some did not arrive at matches, while others went to the wrong grounds.

Somehow, the pools companies managed without the correct information, discovered who was playing whom and the lists were complete and correct.

Eventually, the League and the pools companies became allies, after the League changed its policy.

A match of two games

In 1885 Arbroath beat their opponents by a massive 36–0, but they did have an advantage, because the opposition was the wrong team from the wrong game: they were cricketers.

Arbroath had mistakenly invited Orion Cricket Club to play a game of football, instead of Orion FC of Aberdeen.

The cricket club sportingly made the effort, despite having neither football strip nor boots, and seemed to enjoy the game, even if fate had bowled them a googly.

Climb to victory

Millwall were leading 1–0 against Walsall in November 1948, when their goalkeeper, Malcolm Finlayson, suffered a head injury and was taken to a local hospital. After a check-up he was told he would be all right to go back in goal.

When Finlayson and a Millwall director returned to the ground, however, they found that all the entrances were locked and there was no way of getting in unless they climbed the perimeter wall, which is just what they did.

Finlayson returned to the game when Millwall were 3–1 down, but helped his team to a surprising recovery, winning 6–5.

Mean sheen

It is a poor workman who blames his tools, but in the 1927 FA Cup Final, the goalkeeper managed to blame his jersey.

The deciding shot of the match came from Cardiff's Hugh Ferguson, but it managed to slip through the arms of the Arsenal goalkeeper, Dan Lewis, a Welsh international. Officials decided that the new jersey Lewis was wearing still had its sheen, and in future all new goalkeepers' jerseys had to be softened in the wash before anyone was allowed to wear them on a match day.

Making a fist of it

Injured Denis Law had to sit out Manchester United's
1968 European Cup semi-final with Real Madrid
because of injury. When Bill Foulkes scored for United,
Law punched the air in delight, forgetting about the
low ceiling on the dugout.

His fist went through the plaster, and he was injured
for even longer while he nursed a broken bone in his
hand.

Spectator sport

Northwich Victoria were only able to field eight players
for a GM Vauxhall Conference match against Maidstone
United in November 1986. So Northwich's chairman
Derek Nuttall addressed the crowd over the PA system
to ask whether any of the 738 spectators wanted to play.

To Nuttall's amazement, three volunteers came
forward – Mark Fogg, Steve Garnett and Rick Parkin.

As Northwich were in a fix, they could not be choosy
about whom they sent on to the field, they failed to find
out that one of the three volunteers had consumed a
pork pie and a couple of pints of beer before arriving at
the game.

Despite their handicap, Northwich still managed a 1–1
draw.

Oddballs

The one that (he wished had) got away

This is the tale of a fisherman who probably would have wished his catch had been the one that got away.

On a fishing expedition in 1996, Franc Filipic caught a big one and was determined that this would be the one that would make his career. Unfortunately for the forty-seven-year-old from Ljubljana, Slovenia, he had caught a powerful specimen known as a sheatfish, similar to a catfish.

According to the state-run news agency, the fish pulled Franc under as he uttered his last words: 'Now I've got him!' His body was found after a two-day search.

The fish got away.

A devil of a deep blue sea

Not so much slip-ups as slippery customers befell the Volvo Ocean Race – a round-the-world event that began in Southampton in 2001.

It was reported in early 2002 that sailors were being 'attacked' by flying fish. The Australian sailor Anthony Nossiter was hit in the forehead by a fish measuring 25 centimetres.

Some of the Swedish competitors on the Rio-to-Miami leg were taking bets on who would be the first to catch one and eat it raw. It is not known whether anyone rose to the challenge, but no one seemed too keen.

Everyone's a winner, baby

In the figure-skating competition at the 2002 Winter Olympics in Salt Lake City, huge controversy arose over a decision by a French judge to give her mark to the Russian pair, with the result that not one but two golds were awarded – one to the Russians and one to the Canadians.

The performance of the Russians, Yelena Berezhanaya and Anton Sikharulidze, was generally considered to be inferior to that of the Canadians, Jamie Sale and David Pelletier.

However, the French judge, Marie-Reine Le Gougne, seemed to disagree, and it was discovered that she had had pressure applied to favour the Russians. So there was uproar when it was clearly thought in all quarters that the Canadian pair should have been awarded the coveted prize.

An International Olympic Committee spokesperson said, 'The executive board has followed the International Skating Union proposal to award two gold medals and the votes of the French judge have been cancelled . . .'

The IOC president Jacques Rogge said it was 'in the interests of the athletes'.

The scandal was dubbed, predictably, 'Skategate' by the tabloid media.

It's a gas!

At an ice hockey game between Olympia Heist and Griffoen Geel in Belgium in February 2002, players began to leave the ice, one by one, and so the disgruntled and confused audience responded with boos and shouts, believing the players to be giving in and giving up.

At the time of the first player's departure, Griffoen Geel were being beaten 6–3, which further fuelled the spectators' anger. Later in the game, however, fans began to leave too, feeling weak and ill.

After an investigation, it was discovered that the machine used for clearing the ice between matches had been pumping carbon monoxide out into the stadium. A stadium spokesman told reporters, 'They were shouted at, because everybody thought the players couldn't accept they were losing.'

About 150 people in all needed hospital treatment: 112 managed to drive to the local hospital in Geel, while the others were taken by ambulance. It was left to the local fire brigade to check the stadium and eventually find the faulty machine.

Blast it!

A Canadian angler who was fishing in one of the country's many lakes was thrilled when he found that he had landed an enormous pike. He quickly dispatched it with a stick and laid it on the bank beside his shotgun.

However, the fish was not as dead as the angler thought and began to thrash about. Its tail caught on the trigger and . . . It is not difficult to guess what happened next.

Whether the fish managed to thrash itself back into the water, it will never be known, but the luckless angler did not live to tell the tale.

Victory fit for a king

In 1973, Bobby Riggs displayed overt male chauvinist tendencies when he challenged Billie Jean King to a tennis match that would be a battle of the sexes.

Riggs had last been a Wimbledon champion in 1939, thirty-four years previously, but he was determined to beat this particular member of the sex that, he said, were at their prettiest when barefoot, pregnant, taking care of the children and working in the home.

'I want to set women's lib back twenty years, to get women back in the home where they belong,' he declared. 'I will scrape her up. She is a woman and is subject to women's emotional frailties. She will crack up during the match.'

And so the largest crowd in tennis history so far – about 39,000 – gathered to watch the match. King thrashed him 6–4, 6–3, 6–3.

Untimely

During the 1981 World Snooker Team Cup, the referee, John Smyth, decided he needed a new battery for his travelling alarm clock. He then pocketed the clock, complete with new battery, and forgot about it.

Then, while Smyth was refereeing a match between John Spencer and Paddy Morgan, the alarm clock sprung into life, causing play to be stopped while Smyth hurriedly located the off-switch.

Snapped – and out of it

At the 1956 Melbourne Olympics, it was a stray photographer that caused Britain's cyclists to settle for second place in the team time trial. Billy Holmes crashed into the photographer, who had wandered aimlessly on to the course, damaging his wheel.

Having to change the wheel meant the team lost valuable time, and ultimately they missed first place by just one second.

Weighty problem

A New Zealand bank clerk called Graham May had prepared well for his part in the super-heavyweight category of the weightlifting events at the 1974 Commonwealth Games.

The twenty-one-year-old was about to make a huge lift of 187.5 kilograms. However, as he jerked the bar over his head he suffered a minor blackout and fell from the stage to the floor of the hall.

The weight also fell, and having had some momentum, it careered across the floor, sending officials and spectators running for cover. May soon recovered and took gold.

Mets met with meteoric disaster

The New York Mets baseball team was formed in 1962.
Before their first ever match they received a traditional
American tickertape welcome down Broadway, with
40,000 spectators and a band.

When they did come to
play, they had lost nine games
in a row within a week, a run
of losses matched only by the
Brooklyn Dodgers in 1918.
The Mets went on to lose
more matches in one season
than anyone else in the
history of the game, with a
final figure of 120 defeats.

Troubled waters

It was the occasion of the National Ambulance Service
fishing championships at Kidderminster, Herefordshire,
in 1972. But organizers had forgotten to inform the 200
expected participants of one vital fact.

On the appointed day, the anglers turned up and cast
their lines. All day they sat, and not one of them got a
bite. Eventually a passer-by informed them that they
were wasting their time; the fish had all been moved to
other waters three weeks before.

Hot and bothered

In a misguided effort to cool himself down during the
1950 Tour de France, cyclist Abd-el Kader Zaag drank a
bottle of wine and promptly fell off his bike.

Having slept off his alcohol-induced torpor by the
roadside, he climbed back into the saddle and sped off in
the wrong direction.

All Michael O'Mara titles are available by post from:

Bookpost, PO Box 29, Douglas, Isle of Man, IM99 1BQ

Credit cards accepted.
Telephone: 01624 677237
Fax: 01624 670923
Email: bookshop@enterprise.net
Internet: www.bookpost.co.uk

Free postage and packing in the UK.

Other Michael O'Mara Humour titles:

All Men Are Bastards – ISBN 1-85479-387-X pb £3.99
The Book of Urban Legends – ISBN 1-85479-932-0 pb £3.99
Born for the Job – ISBN 1-84317-099-X pb £5.99
The Complete Book of Farting – ISBN 1-85479-440-X pb £4.99
The Ultimate Book of Farting – ISBN 1-85479-596-1 hb £5.99
The Ultimate Insult – ISBN 1-85479-288-1 pb £5.99
Wicked Cockney Rhyming Slang – ISBN 1-85479-386-1 pb £3.99
Wicked Geordie English – ISBN 1-85479-342-X pb £3.99
Wicked Scouse English – ISBN 1-84317-006-X pb £3.99
The Wicked Wit of Jane Austen – ISBN 1-85479-652-6 hb £9.99
The Wicked Wit of Winston Churchill – ISBN 1-85479-529-5 hb £9.99
The Wicked Wit of Oscar Wilde – ISBN 1-85479-542-2 hb £9.99
The World's Stupidest Criminals – ISBN 1-85479-879-0 pb £3.99
The World's Stupidest Graffiti – ISBN 1-85479-876-6 pb £3.99
The World's Stupidest Laws – ISBN 1-85479-549-X pb £3.99
The World's Stupidest Men – ISBN 1-85479-508-2 pb £3.99
The World's Stupidest Signs – ISBN 1-85479-555-4 pb £3.99
More of the World's Stupidest Signs – ISBN 1-84317-032-9 pb £4.99
The World's Stupidest Last Words – ISBN 1-84317-021-3 pb £4.99
The World's Stupidest Inventions – ISBN 1-84317-036-1 pb £5.99
The World's Stupidest Instructions – ISBN 1-84317-078-7 pb £4.99
Shite's Unoriginal Miscellany – ISBN 1-84317-064-7 hb £9.99
Cricket: It's A Funny Old Game – ISBN 1-84317-090-6 pb £4.99
Football: It's A Funny Old Game – ISBN 1-84317-091-4 pb £4.99